HEAL ME

Insights from the Kabbalistic Tradition

by

Gedaliah Fleer

ISBN-10: 1541213793
ISBN-13: 9781541213791

If you want to know more than you already understand,
you must become more than you already are.

Gedaliah Fleer

In memory of my mother

Rose Fleer

who believed in what I might yet become,
despite my many failings;
her light continues to illuminate and alleviate

ACKNOWLEDGEMENTS

I am exceedingly grateful to all those who read and re-read this book at various stages of its development. In particular, I would like to thank Rabbi Mark Kunis, Barbara Kivowitz, Susan Podziba and Ron Kane. Their insightfulness, criticism and praise guided and encouraged me throughout.

Special thanks to Uriela Sagiv, writer and editor extraordinaire; Ben Gasner, master of graphic design; Diana Korzenik, advisor, support-giver and confidante; and Chana Shapiro whose keen eye and good judgment brought it all together.

Last, but by no means least, I would like to express my admiration and gratitude to my wife Rachel Bracha (Joanie) for taking a semi-completed manuscript out of mothballs and encouraging me to finish what I started. Her love and patience continue to be an undying source of inspiration.

Ultimately, however, after all has been acknowledged, I thank God for every blessing and opportunity.

Gedaliah Fleer

TABLE OF CONTENTS

FOREWORD

Rabbi Gedaliah Fleer is a traditional rabbi with a gentle demeanor whose deep expression of loving-kindness is ever present. He also has a towering intellect and is a visionary Kabbalist and accomplished Talmudist. Until the publication of this book, he was mostly accessible to audiences who attended his talks across the globe.

The publication of this reflection on healing distills his many talks into a startling single volume. As he does in his talks, Rabbi Fleer writes in the Jewish tradition, but the ideas presented here are easily comprehensible by non-Jews, atheists, and anyone who has struggled to heal. He uses the blueprint of Kabbalah – the Jewish map of the process of the universe's creation and sustainment – to describe the inner truths of an individual person. For Kabbalah, the cosmic macrocosm and personal microcosm adhere to identical principles.

Following the Hassidic tradition of Rabbi Nachman of Breslov, Rabbi Fleer tells revealing stories that point his readers toward depths and feelings that we all may have glimpsed but couldn't quite grasp. He also inserts contemporary guided imagery practices that start from a very simple place and take us where we could barely have imagined.

This book speaks with many voices, on multiple levels, and can be read over and over. A meditation on healing, it can help each one of us find a place of deep renewal and healing.

Healing implies a process of regaining intactness, integrity and authenticity, or what Rabbi Fleer calls experiencing the "undifferentiated wholeness" of the "vacated sacred space." The macrocosmic vacated space is central to the divine creation and the "unity of the divine light," and the soul of a person is the divine equivalent within. This primordial space always has possibilities of movement, transformation and rejuvenation. For Rabbi Fleer "every present and immediate moment carries in itself healing power."

Basic to Rabbi Fleer's view of healing is paradox. One of the key contradictions discussed in this book is the need to hope, affirm life and do everything possible to recover, while simultaneously, with the same intensity, putting everything in God's hands, somehow finding an abiding equanimity to accept the fact that recovery may not happen. Both must be true at the same time.

The vacated sacred inner space holds all possibilities. Its emptiness embraces all. It opens us to healing. Maybe this is what Chinese medicine means by what it calls the undifferentiated "essence" (jing) of the "yang assertive will" and the "yin acquiescing will" that allows for all manifestations.

Rabbi Fleer helps us feel this space with words, images, stories and textual quotes. Ultimately, he brings us to a state of intuition and resonance with all the latent potentialities existing in what he calls the "wholeness of undifferentiated unity." His intellectual presentation frees our intuition and activates our inner eye.

Rabbi Fleer explains that absolute unity can never be fully grasped or described and must be felt as a sensibility that opens us to the deepest truths.

This book leaves us with something that is hopeful, palpable and compelling. This is healing.

Ted Kaptchuk
Professor of Medicine, Harvard Medical School
Author of *The Web That Has No Weaver*

INTRODUCTION
Learning to Access the Power to Heal

The mystics teach us that to the extent to which we are open to healing, we will be healed.[1] And therein lies the crux of the problem with illness in our time.

Most of us don't know how to open ourselves, even if we seem to know perfectly well how to close ourselves. But, if we cannot create a space within ourselves in which healing can take place, then it isn't going to happen. So we must learn to develop the ability and strength to remove the obstacles that stand in the way of that process.

In this book we are going to examine how to do exactly that – how to remove the blocks and create a space for healing from whatever ails us and causes us suffering.

There is no one alive to whom suffering is a total stranger. In one way or another we have all experienced what it means to suffer. Is there anyone who has never been injured in a fall, bedridden by disease, betrayed by a once-trusted friend, overwhelmed by responsibility, or devastated by the loss of a loved one? Or perhaps the problem was and continues to be difficult children, a deteriorating marriage, or the ability to simply make ends meet. Given all that can go wrong in life, we never know how, why or when our next encounter with suffering may take place.

While, on the surface, this book is addressed primarily to those suffering from physical ailments, every insight contained herein can easily be transposed to provide objectivity, comfort, transcendence and enlightenment – not all at once, but in due course – to any situation in need of healing. The healing process would happen quite naturally were it not for the fact that we close off those natural possibilities. We do this on many levels. We cut ourselves off not only from healing but from everything around us that normally nurtures us and provides our continual well-being. This is why, when confronted with suffering or illness, mystics ask, "To what extent did my own attitudes induce my illness? How do they slow down my recovery?" They do not ask, "What did I eat?" They ask, "What have I done?"[2]And "What must I do differently? What is this illness teaching me?"

Often people become trapped in psychological states of being that are not healthy, and if they don't free themselves, those negative states of being will ultimately produce in them concrete, physical forms of illness.

Others may be in transition – moving from a negative state of mind to a positive state of mind – and, sometimes, illness becomes a teaching tool in that process. But, they may be resisting learning the psychological lesson that they need to learn from their illness, holding on to negativity because it is familiar and difficult to part with. To the extent that they resist and don't want to learn, the healing will take longer.

And there are those who have been diagnosed with a debilitating disease that could be cured with conventional medicine. But they create within themselves some sort of a psychological blockage that prevents the medication from doing its job.

So this book is for many different types of people – all of us who find that we have to unblock whatever is necessary on a level of spirit or mind that inhibits our ability to heal.

Mystical traditions generally assume that "as above so below" – that is, the spiritual realm above is reflected in the physical realm below and vice versa. The mystical tradition I am going to draw upon here is the

Kabbalah. Although much written about it of late, the Kabbalah is vastly misunderstood, largely because it is so complicated.

To explain simply, the Kabbalah is a Jewish mystical model of all existence. The Kabbalah does not stand alone; rather its wisdom is wholly dependent on the Torah, by which I mean the sum-total of Divine revelation, both written and oral, which happened some 3,300 years ago at Mount Sinai.[3] If we would understand certain basic aspects of the Kabbalistic model – such as the "context" necessary for creation, or the process through which the universe is nurtured and sustained – then we would understand what makes life tick. And then we could use that understanding to heal whatever has caused our lives to fall out of sync with the principles of life that sustain creation.

Therefore, in this book, we will examine certain aspects of the Kabbalistic model, particularly those that explain how the universe came into existence, and how life was made manifest and is perpetuated. If we can do that and then adapt those basic tenets and principles to the way in which we live and deal with illness, we will have discovered something unique that will, hopefully, provide a context for continued life, nurturing and healing.

How is it possible to take something so profound, and all encompassing – universal laws responsible for putting into motion a hundred billion galaxies, each containing a hundred billion stars – and bring it to bear on one individual with a seemingly tiny problem in comparison to the whole of existence?

It is possible because the great heavenly bodies and our bodies here on earth were created to adhere to identical principles, which is exactly what the Kabbalistic model explains.

To use a simple metaphor, let's consider the wheel, which operates on certain basic physical principles. The wheel can be used to make a millstone for grinding wheat or it can be used to make the gears of a wristwatch, a fraction of the millstone's size. The principle of the wheel is the same in both instances – something round that can be set in motion. It is a concept that can help us invent objects to grind wheat, to drive a car, to tell time… The possibilities are endless.

The same dynamic appears at the heart of varying

processes which, in their physical manifestations, do not resemble each other at all.

The Kabbalah seeks to highlight basic concepts of this kind, so as to understand the primal processes that govern the totality of relationships in the physical world and their counterparts in the spiritual realm. When we grasp what the Kabbalah has to teach us, we attain a truly holistic understanding of life. This enables us to move freely from esoteric philosophical concepts – such as God's foreknowledge versus freedom of choice – to an understanding of the necessary tensions which must exist in order for life to come into being and be nurtured in a healthy way. Indeed, a Kabbalistic understanding of how choice works in the universe affords us greater insight into the specific choices we have in life.

Thus we learn that choice does not revolve around something happening or not, rather it revolves around how something happens and when, or over what period of time. According to the Kabbalah, what God wants will ultimately be, but whether it will happen over a short period of time and in ways that are good and pleasant, or over a long period of time in ways that are very unpleasant, that depends on the choices that we make.4 A truly integrated, holistic understanding of the primary processes in the universe must include a profound sensitivity to the "space" in which the universe was created and is maintained.

All too often people are more concerned with what happens in a particular space than the nature of the space itself. But the Kabbalah teaches us that the context in which something takes place is ultimately more powerful than anything that can happen in its midst.5 So let us begin by looking at the mystical doctrine of sacred space, its creation and maintenance. This, according to the Kabbalah, is the fundamental prerequisite for all healing.

PART ONE

SACRED SPACE:
ITS CREATION AND MAINTENANCE

1

Understanding Sacred Space

The first instance where the notion of sacred space is mentioned in the Torah – and from which the Kabbalah draws many insights – is right at the beginning of the story of creation.

We learn in the opening sentences of the Book of Genesis that the entire universe was covered by water, and that God commanded the water to gather into one place.[6]

And immediately we see that a mystical understanding is necessary for what is happening here. For on the face of it, the story does not make sense. The whole world is covered with water, and yet God commands the water to gather in "one place." But is not that "one place" itself already filled with water?

Thus we have our first hint of "sacred space," which, according to the Kabbalists, is a place that contains more than it should be able to hold and that is not diminished by what it contains.[7]

If I have a glass filled with water, I can't put more water into it without first emptying the glass. But if that glass is sacred space, I can put an ocean in there and it won't overflow.

Generally speaking, people tend to think of sacred space as any place where one can find inner peace or where one is able to achieve a sense of transcendence. It could be a beautiful place in the country, it could be a quiet place of learning, or a place of prayer. But for the Kabbalists to call a given space sacred space, it must adhere to very specific criteria and, interestingly, such criteria are made manifest on a regular basis in the workings of the human mind.

The mind is always able to absorb more than it has absorbed already and it is not diminished by what it contains. One cannot say, "I have so much in my mind that nothing else can fit in." We continue to absorb more information as long as we live.

However, the sacred space of the human mind is only as limitless as we allow it to be. That is to say, the fluidity of the mind can come to a grinding halt whenever we let ourselves be intimidated by something we know.

In illness this can readily happen. If you find out that you have a terminal disease and are likely to die, and you begin to accept this as absolute fact, then nothing else is possible. As soon as you allow that kind of negativity into your being, the fluidity of the mind process becomes blocked.

The doctor says, "You have six months left to live," and the patient thinks that the doctor is very wise. He has years of training under his belt, he is a specialist and expert in his field, so he must know. "If the doctor says I have six months to live, then I only have six months to live."

As soon as the patient accepts what his or her doctor has said as absolute and irrefutable, all that could have been achieved through the power of the patient's limitless mind is instantly blocked, shut down by that one single idea: "You will die."

Of course, we will all die eventually, and for that patient the time might be now, but even then – as long as the mind still has the capacity to flow – healing can be brought to bear on how the patient deals with the possibility of death. But if the doctor's words stop the flow, then his sixty-second pronouncement becomes a guaranteed death sentence. That patient will die. There is no hope, no realistic possibility for survival, no future. The limitless life-giving potential of the mind can be short-circuited by that doctor's tersely-worded opinion in the same way that Mt. Everest, a 30,000-foot mountain, can be blocked out by putting an eight-inch hand in front of one's eyes.

The Trap of the Familiar

The mind is a place of transition, one often compared to the ladder in Jacob's dream, which according to its description was "a ladder set up on earth, its top reaching into the heaven with angels of God going up and down on it."[8] Similarly, consciousness of the mind bridges the gap between earth and heaven, raising the physical to recognize its source in transcendence while bringing down the spiritual to give meaning to the mundane. But the sacred space of the mind, which allows consciousness to function without interference, must be safeguarded in spiritual purity.

Spiritual purity is a complex subject, but for our purposes it will suffice to say that in order to safeguard sacred space in spiritual purity, we must continue to nurture within ourselves a context capable of drawing to itself an infinite number of alternatives and potentialities. Interestingly, the Hebrew word for "spiritual purity" (tahor) is closely related to the word for "light" (tihar).[9] And so purity is light. Light flows and illuminates context; light is nurturing; light is life-giving.

On the other hand, the Hebrew word meaning "to make impure" (mitamtame) is closely related to the word meaning "to stuff up" or "to make stupid" (timtam). Thus we find that to clog or stuff up a sacred space is to make it spiritually impure.

Similarly, when the mind's fluidity becomes dammed up, we shut down our awareness of new potentialities, and we literally make ourselves stupid.

There must be room for the possibility of healing. Thus, the first step in any healing process is to create within ourselves a sacred space, a place of purity, a place of light, a place of fluidity, flexibility. The mind cannot be clogged up, shut down. It must continue to flow.

So what is it that clogs us up and shuts us off from the limitless possibilities of our mind?

For one thing, we tend to cling to the familiar. But sometimes familiar things are painful and unhealthy. Still, we cling to them since what is familiar affords us a certain amount of security.

Psychoanalyst Rollo May illustrates this phenomenon by drawing attention to the way mime theater tricks the mind.[10]

Imagine Marcel Marceau doing his act – let's say he is pretending that he's walking a dog. There is no dog, but the way he mimes it – the way he is walking around, straining against the leash – we see the dog, we see the leash, we see a man walking a dog. To us, they are as real as anything that actually exists, but nothing is there. It is because, when he makes the right gestures and movements, he triggers within our minds the picture he wants us to see. Put somewhat differently, in the response to a particular stimulus, the mind moves to complete a given picture in a way that is familiar.

Unfortunately, this mechanism can also work against us. When something happens we immediately jump to certain conclusions, because of a familiar association we have with a particular stimulus. But what if a particular stimulus leads to a conclusion that is terrifying? What happens if we make the natural leap and fill in what's missing by visualizing something that takes away all of our hope of ever recovering?

Sometimes, in order to create the space for healing, we have to stop short of finishing the picture in a way that is familiar. We have to learn how to circumvent this mental process so that it doesn't undermine us, so it doesn't block our sacred space, where healing takes place.

My father used to say to me, "The only reason you have a head is to wear a hat." He used to think I was stupid, and he would constantly let me know just how stupid I was. So today I speak to many audiences, and although I know my subject reasonably well, there are occasions when someone will ask me a question to which I cannot readily provide an answer. And then I have to say to that individual, "I don't know, I have to look it up." When that happens, my mind leaps to a picture of my father saying, "I told you, you only have a head to wear a hat." There was a time when that picture could shake my confidence, but now-a-days, I just smile. The picture is still there, but it has lost its power to intimidate me.

We can't always unload all the negative baggage that we carry, but we can learn to nullify its effect on us so that it no longer causes us pain and doesn't block us.

All too often, the unconscious mind clings to pain that damages our self-image, the kind of pain that comes from guilt or shame, or vulnerability. We all have such baggage. We all have unconscious agendas.

In the conscious world, on the other hand, we yearn for things that make us feel good and secure, give us recognition, are pleasant and consistent with accepted social values and concerns. On a conscious level, we want to advance ourselves, go with the flow, do what's expected of us and do it well. But on an unconscious level, we want to give credence to our negative instincts and fears; it's as if we want to prove them right. Why this is we will soon see.

Once we liberate our consciousness from its negative

dependence on the unconscious familiar, we can go on to deal with other aspects of our psychology that block the fluidity of the mind. But this must be the first step.

2

Liberating Memory

If someone hits you, it hurts. At the moment it happens you have an experience of pain, and it is real. But if the pain experience happened twenty years ago, yet you feel the pain now each time a stimulus triggers the memory, then the pain you are experiencing is not true in terms of your present physical context.

So, for example, let us suppose that as a child you were constantly beaten by a drunkard father. Now you are twenty-years-old, a half-back on your college football team and you tower over your father, who is a short puny fellow. If you wanted to, you could pick him up with one hand and throw him out the window. Yet, when your father starts to yell at you, you are instantly terrified of him, because the real pain you suffered as a child has been re-stimulated. It is no longer real. You have no real cause to be afraid of your father; you are no longer physically vulnerable to him. But in your unconscious mind, your father's power to hurt you has been mythologized. And you feel the same emotional pain and fear you felt as a child. Your father has done nothing to you now; he can't do anything other than trigger an old memory. The pain you are experiencing is outside the present context, but you suffer nevertheless.

This is what it means to be stuffed up, to be overwhelmed by one's baggage. If you were to ask yourself in that moment of terror what you are so anxious about, you'd invariably see that the actual experience of pain happened yesterday – or you are afraid that something similar might happen again tomorrow – but it's not happening now. So, the worry and pain you are carrying around with you has nothing whatsoever to do with your immediate reality.

The only suffering which is real is that which is occurring now, in actual, physical reality. The remembered pain is a phantom. By saying so, I do not mean to de-legitimize emotional pain. From personal experience, I know well how much it hurts. What I am saying is that it needn't be there. If we let pain of the past influence our potentiality in the present, we turn our lives into constant suffering. Every present and immediate moment carries in itself healing power and potential goodness which doesn't deserve to be undermined by past pain that simply doesn't exist in actual objective reality.

Once we become aware of the difference between a current painful experience and a re-stimulated painful experience, we can move on to utilize the potential that exists in every present moment as a means of transcending illness and liberating the sacred space of our unconscious mind.

Perpetuating the Positive

Surprising as it may seem, from a Kabbalistic point of view, the same is not true when it comes to positive experience. A past negative experience that is perpetuated and re-stimulated becomes a monstrous force that can blot out the healing potential of the present. In contrast, a positive experience that is perpetuated and re-stimulated serves to enhance the positive potential of the present.

The negative experience is only true at the moment it occurs. But the positive experience – past or present – is legitimately part of the now. Everything that's positive about yesterday is positive about today.

To understand this spiritual phenomenon we need to recognize that all of creation has one common denominator – everything originates from one source, God. All creation is a manifestation of God's goodness and God's will, and so anything that's consistent with that ongoing reality is true all the time. Anything that's out of sync with that reality is false.

King David gives us profound insight into this idea by telling us: "He who implants the ear, does He not hear? He who designs the eye, does He not see?"[11]

King David is saying that, if God created within us the ability to hear and see, then God too must be able to hear and see. This, of course, does not mean that God has ears and eyes, but rather, whatever God creates must reflect a potential that has a source in Himself.

In other words, everything in creation can teach us something about God. For everything in creation corresponds to some aspect of the Creator, and is nurtured by a life force that reflects the Divine. Everything in the entire universe is connected at its core to God. And, therefore, everything in the universe can be utilized in our quest to access the infinite, to access goodness and healing, to access God.

Because God is the common denominator, any two things can always be compared in some way to each other. For no matter how different their function or form, they share a common life force that is connected to the same source. On some profound level everything, all plurality, flows from the unity that is God.

Therefore, if there's something that's positive and meaningful in my life now, and tomorrow I find it consistent with something new which happens, then that which happens tomorrow will be simply a further elaboration and development of what happened yesterday.

However, this is not true for the negative. If there's something that holds me back, that stifles the fluidity of my thought process, curtails my ability to heal, on any level, then it has no place in the natural flow that's connected to the God-given positive energy holding the world together, from which everything is nurtured, in which everything is united.

In other words, whatever reinforces our connection with our Creator, with the transcendental, is positive, for it flows and empowers and heals. Whatever severs our connection with the transcendental is negative and, if perpetuated, only stifles hope, damages our connection to the life force, and impedes healing.

Therefore, it becomes clear that whatever happened that was negative yesterday can keep us from what's positive today. But what happened that was positive yesterday will naturally reinforce whatever positive potential awaits us tomorrow.

Many of us have had the unfortunate experience of walking into the hospital room of someone who's dying from a terminal disease and, as much as we might have wanted to be comforting and helpful, instead we've found ourselves at a loss for words. Because what can anyone say at such a time? Surely not something stupid like, "Umm, we all have to go sometimes, it's just too bad you have to go now." Anything you might dream up, no matter how truthful, sincere and loving is likely to fall flat on its face at a moment like this. So what do you say in such a situation?

The best thing to do is to reminisce about past positive experiences the two of you have shared. If you do that, you will find that the person will respond, and for a number of reasons. First, the happy reminiscence communicates a certain kind of goodness about life that can never be diminished. You are putting the person who is ill in touch with the essence of a positive experience as it once existed and as it still exists in this moment. Second, and perhaps even more important, because you have such positive memories means that there's something in the nature of your mutual experience that is going to live on beyond the two of you, that you've been the caretakers of, and that you are both still able to communicate to others. You were partners in something that is going to outlive the both of you – it isn't going to die.

In this way the positive reinforces the positive. But the negative only blocks out any possibility of the positive.

I'm not saying that we can't learn or grow from the negative. Obviously, we can learn from negative experiences – indeed, that may well be their purpose in our lives – and by doing so we enrich ourselves and make our futures more profound. But if we don't learn from negative experiences but instead get stuck in them, then the re-stimulated memory can only make us feel guilty or continually vulnerable and bring us pain. That kind of negativity, which only serves to block us, is not constructive; it is not teaching us anything, except perhaps that we must do everything possible to get rid of it.

The Shape of Things to Come

Another thing we must remember is that our beliefs create experience, and not the other way around. If we believe that God runs the world, that His will is manifest in the world, and we seek to establish a relationship with the Divine, then our experiences will serve that belief and reinforce that belief.

But many people feel that it works the other way around – that experience creates what we believe in. If we have bad experiences as children, the reasons for which we don't understand, if bad things happened to us in ways that seemed random, without rhyme or reason, then we are locked into perceiving the world as a horrible place full of land mines set to blow our lives to smithereens. And, of course, then we walk through the world in constant anxiety, and it is a place of fear and apprehension for us.

If this is what one believes, then one's experiences will flow from that belief and serve to reinforce these same beliefs in a circular fashion. In point of fact, whatever the starting point, our beliefs create the experiences that we encounter.

It is also important to understand that form follows function, not the other way around. Gerald Epstein, M.D., a leading pioneer in the field of mind-body medicine, points out that we don't see because we have eyes, but rather having eyes allows us to fulfill the function of seeing.[12] Indeed, we may have eyes and not want to see. So the function of seeing is fulfilled through the presence of organs called eyes. But the fact that we have these eyes doesn't mean that we will see.

People can look directly at something and not see it, because they are not focused, or it went by too quickly, or they subconsciously don't want to see that particular thing. On the other hand, people who lose their sight suddenly find that their other senses are more acutely sensitive. Through those other senses, they are able to pick up cues that create pictures in their mind, and they are able to "see." The function of seeing thus continues, but the way in which things are seen and the organs that make "sight" possible have changed.

Functions are thus transferable from one form to another, but the reverse is not true. So, if a person wants to serve himself, others or God, only by means of a particular form, he may find himself blocked if that form suddenly becomes unavailable to him. A football player who loses a leg in a car accident can no longer play football. If he was only concerned with the form – playing football – as a means of achieving inner satisfaction, then he is finished. But if he was concerned with function – and was, for example, using his physical prowess to express his physical know-how – then he can train others based on his experience and continue to fulfill that function.

In the very same way, our beliefs create and mold our experiences. What we believe in the most fundamental terms about ourselves, our abilities, our potentialities – that is, how we perceive ourselves as human beings in the deepest sense – shapes the outcome of everything we do. We predetermine whether we are going to succeed or fail. Now I am not talking about anything crazy like believing one can fly, or walk on water, or anything like that. I am talking about one's self-image. Do I see myself as a good person or a bad person, a person deserving of good things or a person in need of punishment, a successful person or a failure? The more I strengthen my self-image with the proper sense of belief in my own potential, the more my life experiences will reflect and confirm that image.

What I'm trying to convey here is that if I have a positive self-image, then that self-image can neither be taken away nor bolstered by success or failure. We do not rise and fall with the experiences of a given day. We learn from them and move on, because something else is driving us forward – a healthy self-image whose powerful potential is never dependent on any particular form for its manifestation in the world.

Because you think positively about yourself is no guarantee that you're always going to be successful in whatever you undertake. Nor is success going to impact on your ability to become a better person. Success does not make you better, and the lack of success doesn't make you worse. Your self-image and your belief in yourself tells you that your focus is on using your potential to the best of your ability – fulfilling your function in the best way you know how and letting God run the world. The outcome is not ultimately in your hands, and it does not reflect on your self-worth.

Now, unfortunately, many people do not think this way, because they have not learned to think this way. So, even if these people are highly successful individuals, they will encounter times when they walk into an experience they aren't prepared for. If they allow themselves to be overpowered by that experience and intimidated by it, then that experience will affect and shape what they believe concerning their potential. Once it does that, then the sacred space of the mind is contaminated, it's stuffed up. When one negative experience starts to wield a disproportionate amount of influence, it sets up an exaggerated threat that the same thing can repeat itself in the future.

This is what Epstein calls "if-then" thinking.[13] If x happened, then y must be the outcome. "If-then" thinking is logical. But truth is not always logical. Truth, explains Epstein, "always concerns itself with what is – with what presents itself to us in the immediacy of the present moment. Logical thinking projects into the future, making predictions, drawing conclusions, gauging outcomes [based on past experiences]." Logical thinking does not take into account that the future is pure potential, that the future does not have to be determined by the past, unless we allow it. By taking the past, and using it as a yardstick to gauge or predict the outcome of the future, what we do in fact is limit the possibilities of experience as a result of our own fixed ideas.

We've got to ask ourselves the question: Is what will happen tomorrow already shaped by what I believed was going to happen today – in other words, am I really giving the potential of tomorrow a chance?

The world is not fixed; the world flows. In terms of pure science, we have to recognize that how we understand the condition of humankind changes dramatically every twenty years. How we understand the world today differs nearly completely from how it was understood twenty years ago. Water is still wet, one plus one equals two, and illness is still common. But the way in which we understand the reasons for these things, and are able to demonstrate exceptions to our perceived rules, has changed drastically. In another fifty years our understanding will have changed almost completely from our present understanding. So, to what extent can we accurately predict the future based on our understanding of how things worked in the past or of how things work now? To imprison the possibilities of tomorrow in our fixed notions of yesterday makes about as much sense as encasing the wings of birds in cement or cutting off the legs of a frog and asking it to jump.

The Jumping Frog

I'd like to end this chapter with a humorous tale, which illustrates the pitfalls of this type of reasoning:

It was Friday morning and a biology professor was about to conduct an experiment. His students gathered round him as he proceeded to inject a frog with a local anesthetic so that it would not feel any pain. He then cut off one of the frog's legs and asked it to jump. The frog jumped. The professor then severed a second leg and asked it to jump. When the frog didn't jump, the professor raised his voice and shouted for it to jump. Finally, with the two remaining legs, the frog jumped.

Then, while his students paid close attention, a third leg was removed. Again, the professor asked the frog to jump. He asked and shouted, but it didn't move. Then the students joined in screaming and pounding their fists on the laboratory table. After a while, mustering all of its strength, the frog managed to jump with its one remaining leg.

The professor then cut off the last of the frog's legs and asked it to jump. But this time, despite the calls and cries of teacher and students, and the sounds of their fists on the table, the frog did not jump.

The professor then asked his students to write up this experiment over the weekend. And, for each of them to include in his or her report what they thought this experiment proved.

On Monday morning, the students returned to class. They had all come to the same conclusion. When a frog loses all of its legs, it goes deaf.

3

Getting Rid of Old Pain

In order to create sacred space in which healing can take place, we must, in every possible way, rid ourselves of old remembered pain that clogs us up. This is easier said than done, because most people seem to hold onto such pain for dear life. And they cannot explain why.

There are many reasons why we hold onto old pain, but a few are universal:

First, we tell ourselves that if we can remember the terrible things that happened, then we'll be protected against similar things happening again. If we were to forget how painful a past experience was, then we might let our guard down, become that vulnerable again or that stupid again, and allow that kind of experience to repeat itself. Therefore, we convince ourselves that as long as we keep the old pain fresh in our memories, we are protected. The problem with that kind of thinking, besides the obvious constant re-living of bad experiences, is that we are constantly feeding ourselves the message that we are weak and in need of protection.

A second reason we cling to old pain is that it is a way of validating our suffering. By recalling past pain, we confirm the fact that something terrible happened to us in the past and, therefore, our present suffering is legitimate. Thus the past bad experience becomes a constant excuse for all sorts of failings. Now we can say: "What do you want from me, I'm damaged. My mother hit me on my head when I was three years old, and my father never loved me. How could I grow up to be anything but a failure?"

A third reason why we hold onto pain is that remembering it is a way of telling ourselves we are good. The one who inflicted the pain was bad; we did nothing to deserve it. This is clearly true if we were small, innocent children, but adults often can't make that claim. We don't want to admit that, on some level, we might also have had something to do with what happened to us. Therefore, we insist that we are completely good, and the perpetrator was completely bad. In that way we do not have to accept any responsibility for what went wrong.

The fourth reason we cling to pain is the opposite of the above. Instead of refusing to admit responsibility, we take on responsibility that is not ours. That is called misplaced guilt. If we were abused as children, the abuses we suffered were not our fault in the least. But we can't forgive ourselves for having been vulnerable. Remembering the pain is a way of staying in the mindset of that totally defenseless, vulnerable child and, by doing so, we nurture within ourselves the potential for vulnerability. We fear that we could slip up and be that vulnerable again. And, of course, if we remain in the mindset of a vulnerable child, that is exactly what we will continue to be in the depths of our heart.

Finally, there are those of us who can't get rid of old pain because we totally identify with it. We think, erroneously, that we have become our pain; it is who we are. We say: "I can't get rid of my pain, I don't want to get rid of my pain. My pain is so deep, it's so much a part of who I am that getting rid of my pain would be like cutting out a piece of my soul." This is totally unreasonable, because if it were really true, if I and my pain were one and the same in the deepest sense, then I wouldn't be able to perceive that I am in pain. In order to be in pain, in order to say something hurts, or something is embarrassing, or something is terrifying, I have to be able to look at the pain from the outside and identify it.

There has to be something whole in me that retains objectivity, a part of me that hasn't been hurt, that retains a notion of what light is, and that is capable of identifying the darkness that I am experiencing as pain. There has to be some aspect of myself that knows with clarity and certainty that the pain I am feeling is not part of my essential being. For if the totality of who I am literally merged with the pain, then there would be nothing to compare that pain with, no way to draw distinction between light (absence of pain) and darkness (presence of pain); there would be no way for me to know and recognize my pain. I would be like a child who was born blind who can't know that he is blind, not having known any other condition.

Forgiving One's Self

When we cling to old pain, there is always a part of us that is fighting the experience. There is a part of us that is healthy and does not want to reopen old wounds over and over again, and this part of us is terribly disturbed because it's not being heard. This part of us feels imprisoned in a hard outer shell built up of past loss, past pain, past horrors. The only way to break out of that shell is through forgiveness.

Whenever I speak about forgiveness, someone in the audience invariably brings up the Holocaust, in order to show me that there are things that are unforgivable, and that being the case, there may be individual experiences that are unforgivable as well.

In answer to such a question I remind people that forgiveness is a two-way street. I can decide not to hold a grudge, but actual forgiveness requires the active participation of the person who caused me to suffer. If that person does not ask my forgiveness, does not resolve never to repeat such behavior again, and makes no amends for his or her wrongdoing to whatever extent is possible, then my forgiveness is meaningless. Thus, in terms of the Holocaust, I cannot forgive the pain caused to others.

Only those who suffered themselves can choose not to hold a grudge. In so far as the German people are concerned, I can forget the deeds of their fathers when dealing with the new generation. However, I find the fact that they are too ready to forget is difficult for me to forgive. Only time will prove their intentions.

All of this, however, has little to do with our discussion. For we are not talking here of the legal or moral definition of forgiveness which involves the active participation of the person who wronged us. Instead, we are referring to a kind of forgiveness that must be attained in order to free ourselves from the negative influence of past pain.

We cannot be rid of pain carried inside of ourselves unless we learn to forgive ourselves for having once been vulnerable. I am not saying that vulnerability is something to be ashamed of. To the contrary – sensitivity and vulnerability are some of the loftiest qualities of the human condition. But there are aspects of our vulnerability that have been abused, causing us to doubt our inner strength, integrity and self-worth. It is this negative sense of vulnerability that we must

overcome in ourselves through forgiveness. The cause
of that vulnerability – whether it was something we
brought on by ourselves as adults or whether we were
simply defenseless children who had nothing at all to
do with what happened – doesn't really matter. We
must find in our hearts the strength to forgive ourselves.
If we can't, then the pain we harbor will continue to
dominate our lives forever. But if we can, then what will
happen as a result of that forgiveness is a change in our
perception of the past. For one thing, we will no longer
see the person that hurt us as completely evil.
We will see his or her actions as evil, but we won't
equate the pain that he or she inflicted with the totality
of that person.

If we can make this distinction in ourselves – between
who we are in terms of our essential being and who we
are in terms of our vulnerability or wrongdoings – then
we stand a good chance of ridding ourselves of the
negative influence of past pain and shaking off the hard
shell that stifles us. Then, our true self and its limitless
potential will no longer be intimidated by the fact that
we were once vulnerable in a negative way. And we will
come to disassociate our core from any manifestation of
our weaknesses. Only then can we forgive ourselves for

having once been vulnerable and get on with our life in a productive way.

When we forgive ourselves for having been vulnerable, we create within ourselves a sacred space in which our thought process can flourish. We release our mind from the hold that the past has on it and liberate the countless possibilities that can heal and shape our future in positive ways. Now we can be in the unobstructed present and receive from the potentiality of every moment contained in the present.

The essence of getting rid of pain is this ability to forgive ourselves. But in order to do that, we must be willing to sacrifice. Sacrifice is a necessary prerequisite to healing, as it is a necessary prerequisite for creating sacred space. In order to create sacred space, we have to sacrifice negativity, we have to get rid of whatever contaminates that space, pollutes the space, stuffs it up.

It is interesting that in Hebrew the word for "sacrifice" is korban, which comes from the same root as karev, meaning "to draw near." In order to draw near to something that's transcendental we have to sacrifice something that's physical.

To sacrifice in the deepest sense means to let go of whatever is standing in the way of our limitless potential, and for many of us that means whatever it is that's causing us pain.

This can be a very subtle business. It is easier when the kind of pain we suffer has an identifiable source, be it emotional or physical. But there are many other kinds of buried pain. Sometimes we are hardly aware that the pain is there. We are just restless and unhappy, but we would not call what we feel "suffering." Yet we suffer none-the-less because this nameless obstacle is preventing us from becoming more than we are, from achieving our limitless potential. And to achieve it may mean that we have to sacrifice the so-called "good life." It is not a good life at all when it is repetitive, predictable and it is going nowhere; we'd feel so much lighter and more fluid if we could just leave this "good life" behind. But it can be a very difficult sacrifice to make when the price is loss of comfort, money, status or security.

In the 1960s, there were successful artists who were getting $50,000 to $100,000 per painting, and they would show up at Berkeley, the Mecca of the Love

Generation, and burn their works. People would try to stop them and say "I'll buy it from you, don't burn it." But they would insist that this is what they had to do: "I have to burn it to go beyond this creative stage." And whatever you might think of their actions, the spirit behind it was correct.

To reach new levels of potential, sacrifice is necessary. Sacrifice can mean letting go of emotional baggage, letting go of old pain, but it can also mean letting go of those things that give us security, those things that we cling to and are afraid to relinquish.

In short, to sacrifice is about making distance, about setting ourselves apart from something. It is through this action of setting apart that sacred space is created.

4

Visualization Exercises for Part One

The reason for the following visualizations is to take what we have been discussing out of the intellectual realm, translating its essence into experience to the extent that this is possible.

Visualizations are best done when one is seated relaxed with eyes closed, while an experienced guide suggests images.

This, of course, is not possible to accomplish through a book, and when one reads through an exercise, the element of surprise that is an essential part of the experience is lost.

Perhaps it would be best, before reading on, to enlist the

help of a friend. And have that friend read to you the following text.

It is important to remember this type of imagery involves a process of free association. If one tries to think about an image, while trying to relate to the image, then the image will have little healing effect because it will lose its spontaneity.

In order for the exercise to be of benefit, close your eyes, breathe out deeply, relax, and let the image flow. Whatever comes to the forefront of your mind first and most naturally is what is real. As soon as you begin to think about what you see or what it means, you contaminate the purity of the image that comes from your subconscious. So give yourself over to the visualizations and let the images flow out of you without thinking.

Wait until you have gone through this process before contemplating what automatically came into your mind.

To help you internalize the lesson of this section, the following two visualizations should prove helpful.

"A"

Close your eyes, and make yourself as comfortable as you can.

Now breathe out deeply, three times.

See yourself standing alone. Your arm is stretched out in front of you and its hand is folded into a fist, tightly closed.

Breathe out.

Now slowly open your hand and see and know what you must let go of in order to be free.

Breathe out and open your eyes.

"B"

Close your eyes, and make yourself as comfortable as you can.

Breathe out deeply, three times.

It's a beautiful spring day, the sun is shining and you're jogging. To your right, alongside the jogging path is a patch of thick green grass, and beyond the grass, further to your right is a stream of fast-flowing, fresh water.

Breathe in the fresh air, smell the grass, feel the sun on your face and hear the movement of the water coming from the stream.

Breathe out.

As you look to your left, you see the person who caused you most pain jogging alongside of you. The two of you continue jogging along the path.

You're both feeling tired now. So you and the other person slow down and stop.

Both of you walk off the path onto the green grass and sit down facing each other, as close as you can get to the stream of fast-flowing, fresh water.

Breathe out.

There are arrows in your heart and you are going to take out those arrows one at a time.

Take out the first arrow and explain to the person sitting opposite you what kind of pain this arrow represents … who put it there … and why you were vulnerable to it.

Then, take the arrow and put it into the stream of fresh, flowing, fast-moving water, and both of you watch as the arrow floats away and disappears.

Now take the second arrow out of your heart. Explain what kind of pain this arrow represents … who put it there … and why you were vulnerable to it.

Then put that second arrow into the stream of fast-flowing, fresh water, and both of you watch as it floats away and disappears.

Do this with each of the arrows in your heart.

Take as much time as you need.

When you have finished, keep your eyes closed but raise your hand to signal the person who is reading this visualization to you so that you can continue on with the exercise.

Breathe out.

Now look and see if there isn't one last arrow still in your heart that has to come out. If there is, take it out, explain it as you did the others, put it into the water and watch it float away.

Breathe out.

Now watch and listen as the person sitting opposite you

takes the arrows out of his or her heart, one at a time, explaining as you did what pain each arrow represents … who put it there … why he or she was vulnerable.

Watch as that person puts each of his or her arrows into the stream of water, where they float away and disappear.

Once this is done, see this person check his or her heart to find out if there is one more arrow that needs to be removed.

If so, watch and listen as he or she removes that last arrow, explains its meaning, puts it into the stream, where it floats away and disappears.

Breathe out.

Now both of you stand up and walk back onto the path and continue jogging. Soon you come to a crossroad – continue jogging. Don't think. If you separate at the crossroad and go in different directions, that's good. But if you stay on the same path, that's also good. Whatever happens is for the best.

Stop jogging.

Breathe out.

Jump from the place you are standing into a beautiful garden.

It's a spring day, the sun is shining, and you can smell the scent of flowers and fruit trees coming into bloom.

Find a peaceful place, lie down on the grass and feel the warmth of the sun on your face.

Breathe out.

Look into your body and see your heart. Notice the bruised areas where the arrows used to be.

Breathe the light of the sun through your clothes and through the pores of your skin into your heart. See and know the sun healing those bruises and restoring your heart.

Breathe out and open your eyes.

PART TWO

THE DYNAMIC OF PARADOX
AND ITS ROLE IN HEALING

1

Accessing Paradox in the Process of Healing

Quantum theory holds that the more one tries to observe a system's state as the system is going through a quantum jump, the more likely that jump will not occur. And, indeed, scientists have been able to carry out successful experiments, showing that the mere act of observing an ion can interfere with its ability to make quantum jumps to higher atomic energy levels.14

This phenomenon has been compared to a pot of water coming to a boiling point. It's almost a joke: "a watched pot never boils." The temperature of the water builds up and up, but when does it jump past the boiling point and bubble? In the quantum realm, it cannot if someone is watching.

So imagine that a human being is looking forward to something, planning and doing what he or she can to make it happen. The project begins to take shape, it assumes a life of its own. Depending on who or how many people are involved, the intensity of their effort sets things in motion. But somehow the project's ultimate goal eludes them. No matter how hard they try, things don't come together and blossom to fruition until the people stop trying so hard and turn their attention away.

In human psychology, we often notice this peculiar phenomena. For example, a woman tries very hard to get pregnant, doing everything imaginable – tests, fertility treatments, praying from dawn to dusk – but it is not until she accepts the possibility she may not have children and turns her attention away, that miraculously she becomes pregnant. It's as if that woman had to say, "I've spent my whole life fantasizing about children, praying for children, going to experts to make it happen, and now I am ready to surrender to God's will. I'll do the next best thing – I'll adopt." And, often, as soon as she is willing to do that she gets pregnant.

Why does this happen?

It happens because she built up the positive energy, and then turned around and accepted the possibility of the exact opposite. She did everything she could to get pregnant, then put it all in God's hands and moved on with her life.

So it is in healing. You must be willing to accept the paradox of wanting with all your heart to get better, but at the same time being willing to turn your attention away, fully accepting the fact that you might not recover.

In my work with terminally ill people, especially cancer patients, I saw how this works. I would come in, get them to relax, close their eyes, and guide them through various visualizations. Typically, we'd concentrate on healthful images, on cancer cells diminishing in number, on blood flowing regularly, and so forth. These visualizations worked healing miracles for some, but for most people nothing happened. And this is the reason why:

If you concentrate on an affirmative image and build up all the healing energy, that healing energy doesn't explode, yield fruit and actually heal, unless you can do a complete about-face and acquiesce to the possibility of death.

You must, with your whole heart, affirm life and, at the same time, accept, with total equanimity, the possibility of death. If you can do that, then the positive healing energy, which you have built up through your affirmative efforts and imagery, may have the chance to explode and bring about healing.

It's a profound idea. You say yes and only yes – yes to life, yes to death – you never say no.

This attitude creates a kind of "vacated space" – a space empty of fixed ideas, a place where healing energy can be nurtured to fruition without being overwhelmed by negativity. [For a detailed exposition of the Kabbalistic understanding of vacated space and how it gives rise to sacred space, see the Appendix.]

In the earlier stages of illness this will work. It gets harder, of course, in the more advanced stages of disease. But even then, this attitude – coming from a deep place of conviction – will relax the patient and cause a certain amount of relief from pain. Whether a cure can be brought about depends on many factors – one's ability to focus, one's will power, one's faith in God, and the ultimate whole-hearted acceptance of the possibility that one might die.

But some people just can't enter the vacated space where anything is possible. They can't acquiesce to paradox.

Without a doubt, the paradox of healing requires a mindset that is unique and sometimes difficult to achieve. On the one hand, you must act as if God isn't there – you must behave as if everything depends on you alone. This means doing everything you know to heal and stay alive, this means having hope, this means getting proper medical treatment, this means making every physical effort to recover. On the other hand, you must acknowledge – at the very same time – that nothing will work unless God wills it. And you must be completely at ease with the possibility that your recovery may not be part of His game plan.

You can't do this because I told you to do it. You have to internalize this idea and believe it completely, which is difficult to do because you must accept two contradictory things at the very same time, equally with the same conviction.

If you try to convince yourself that you are going to heal while a part of you thinks you are going to die, or, if you try to accept death while hanging on to hope in the corner of your heart, healing will not happen.

Acceptance has to be total both ways.

There is an adage, related in the Talmud,15 that "Anyone who runs away from honor, honor pursues him, but anyone who pursues honor, honor runs away from him." A man once came to a rabbi complaining that he had been running away from honor all his life, but somehow it didn't pursue him as the Talmud said it would. The rabbi explained, "Honor is not pursuing you, because you keep turning around to see if it's there and so, after a while, it loses interest."

If you keep turning around to see if the water is boiling, so to speak, it will never bubble up. If you keep turning around watching to see if you are healing, the explosion of healing energy will not take place.

But, if you can access the paradox of healing, you will have entered the vacated space where new creation comes into existence from out of nothing, ex nihilo, and where anything is possible.

On the one hand, it is frightening, like entering an abyss. On the other hand, at virtually the same time, it is a context for new beginning.

Indeed, vacated space stimulates will, since will is a

byproduct of absence. We only yearn for what we know, for things once seen or imagined, for possessions or perhaps experiences gone lost. For, just beneath any sense of loss or absence, there is an awareness of something quite real that must be internally processed and allowed to surface anew. The results are often surprising but bring with them healing and wholeness.

As I yearn for what I know but don't have, I am moved to fill the void I experience, and this impetus to act is will. There is an old adage: "Where there is a will, there is a way." And this is exactly how new beginnings are born.

2

Finding a Cornerstone of Faith

There was once a woman who was pregnant with twins. One twin was an optimist and the other a pessimist. One day, having been in the womb for nearly nine months, the pessimist said to his brother, "It seems to me that we're not going to be in this place much longer. After all, we're growing larger and the space we're in is getting crowded. Either we will suffocate or be forced out of here. No matter what happens, there will be nothing left of us."

His brother, the optimist, remained calm. "It seems to me," he said, that whatever force brought us here didn't do it for nothing. There must be a plan, and though I don't know what it is, I'm sure that we will be taken to a more comfortable location.

The pessimist, in a state of great anxiety, responded, "How can you talk like that? This is the only reality we know. If we were forced from here, how would we survive? We would be cut off from this tube that nurtures us; there would be nothing to keep us in existence. Why do you insist on clinging to such ridiculous fantasies?"

"I don't know," said the optimist. "I just sense that there is a reality beyond the smallness of this space."

As it turned out the optimist was born first. The pessimist could hardly believe his eyes. A moment ago, his brother was right there beside him and, in an instant, he was gone. The pessimist strained to put his ear against the womb. Suddenly, he heard a scream and then there was silence. "You see," he said to himself, "I always knew it, there's nothing left of him."

As our sages teach, "From the moment of birth, we are taught about death."[16]

In the Face of Death

If you are ill, you must find in yourself a point of believing – a cornerstone of faith – where you recognize that you are not looking at the end, but at a possibility for a new beginning.

Unfortunately, people generally think of faith as a last resort. When every reasonable possibility has been exhausted and they want to hold onto hope, they tend to move in the direction of faith. But, in actuality, faith is connected with the continuity of life and with the renewal of potential.

When we have a question, we set out looking for an answer. But as soon as we find it, we tend to stop looking, not realizing that the answer we now rely on has cut us off from any possibility of renewed potential.

The continuity of life and fullness of potential can never be known in their entirety. But as soon as we put all our stock into a particular limiting answer, we have cut ourselves off from any further possibility of discovery.

Science often works that way. A question is answered and a theory is accepted as fact; challengers are rebuffed. But twenty-five years later a brave person comes along and takes a look at the same question from a different angle, and major advances in scientific understanding result.

Every answer at some point is limited. Every answer runs up against something that it should be able to resolve but doesn't. When we acknowledge that, the door to new discovery opens.

This is where faith comes in. Faith is not really a belief in the miraculous. Rather it is a trust that what is presently unknowable or beyond the limits of our experience can be accessed. Faith is simply asking a question, calling out to God and believing an answer will come.

This kind of faith takes a leap – a leap into vacated space, in a manner of speaking.

The faith of which I speak is both blind and informed. That is to say, we must use our powers of reason to understand the limitations of intellect. And thus informed by reason, we can then recognize those situations where we must make a leap of faith beyond reason itself.

There are times when we have to believe in purpose and

possibility, because we intuit that those things are true of everything in creation. We must persist in this belief even when intellectually we have no way of knowing what that purpose or possibility might be.

Those extraordinary people – who entered the gas chambers of Auschwitz knowing they were about to take their last breath, and yet who nevertheless had faith in God and in the purpose of life when nothing seemed to make sense whatsoever – had accessed this realm.

It is the realm of unity with one's source, with God Himself. This is what allowed them to have faith. And faith is the most extreme manifestation of will.

Pure will is "I want." I want to believe there is a God. I want to believe there is a purpose in the face of the Holocaust. I want. I don't need to know why, I don't need to know how. I want, that's all, in the same way that God created the universe because He wanted to, not because He had to. He did it as an act of unconditional love.

And we return that unconditional love when we accept with unconditional faith that we are created in the image of God and that nothing can alter that – not what we might have done wrong, not what is closing in on us, not what illness we might be fighting. The fact that we exist is reason to continue and that in itself is beyond reason.

When empirically there is no reason to continue to believe that I'm going to get better, that doesn't mean that I shouldn't have the will to live.

Once I understand that, I can will myself to transcend the trap of physical space and time that is holding me back. And I can start anew, opening myself to the pure potential of a new beginning.

How can I learn something completely new? How can I open myself to an entirely new experience? I've got to access the paradox and take a leap into pure potential.

Mystics who seek the truth know that the only way they can hope to reach higher planes of knowledge is by opening themselves in an extreme way, by undergoing what is called in meditative circles an "ego-death." And "ego-death" is just a term to describe the clearing out all the baggage so that one has unobstructed access to one's own soul.

This is the challenge before us; indeed this has been the

challenge all along since we began our discussion of sacred space in the earliest pages of this book.

Now that we understand the paradox of healing, we will examine how it is possible for us to access it and make healing real – by tapping into the awesome power of our own soul.

Unless we can get in touch with that aspect of ourselves which was created in the image of God, understanding the paradox of healing will have no effect on us; it will not bring us healing. We may access the paradox on the intellectual level, but to really heal we need to experience it on the highest level where anything is possible – on the ultimate level of soul.

3

Visualization Exercises for Part Two

"A"

Close your eyes, and make yourself as comfortable as you can.

Breathe out deeply, three times.

You see yourself looking into a mirror and you notice that your face is a mask.

Take off the mask and see and know what is underneath.

Having done this, you realize that what you are looking at is also a mask.

So take this second mask off as well and see and know what is underneath.

Then you realize that this, too, is a mask.

So take off this third mask and see what is underneath. Keep doing this until you have taken off all the masks that you are wearing … Slowly, one at a time … until you see and know that in yourself which is in the image of God.

Take a deep breath and open your eyes.

"B"

Close your eyes, and make yourself as comfortable as you can.

Breathe out deeply, three times.

In your mind's eye, look at the sun and feel its warmth on your body.

See and know that the sun represents the healing power of God. Feel its strength, its security.

Breathe the light of the sun into that essence in yourself that is in the image of God.

Breathe out. Turn your eyes inward.

See and know the place in yourself that harbors pain.

Go into that place.

See and know who or what is there generating the pain.

Breathe out.

Breathe from the essence of your being, which is in the image of God, into the place of your pain. See and know your pain being healed by the power of your essence.

If you have any trouble doing this, simply link your Godly essence to the light of the sun. Then breathe your Godly essence, while it is still receiving from the sun, into the place of your pain.

See and know yourself healing.

Take a deep breath, and open your eyes.

PART THREE

THE HEALING POWER OF THE SOUL

1

Soul as Doorway to Potential

Thus far we have examined some deep Kabbalistic concepts that govern healing. But understanding how these profound models operate is not enough. To tap into their power, we must internalize what we have learned. We must elevate our knowledge to the level of experience.

What we know has to become who we are.

The soul is the vehicle through which this is made possible.

Just as the vacated space is the grounding and the context which gives rise to everything that comes into being within itself, so too, there are aspects of soul that serve as the grounding and context that allows for every articulation of itself.

Indeed, the soul on its highest level of manifestation bears the imprint of God's vacated presence. This means that God is in the soul of every person, but in a way that is so hidden that we cannot describe what He is, other than to say that He is the source of all selflessness and longing which emanate from the experience of His vacated presence.

Longing is manifest as will. And will, as we have already begun to discover, is guided by faith through which it is possible to access the highest spiritual level of selflessness.

It is essential to remember that creation ex nihilo is an ongoing process; God constantly generates new life and ever-greater healing potential by virtue of His goodness,[17] which is not dependent or limited by earthly reason or rationale.

Only one who possesses faith can tap into this unconditional goodness, for faith too, is unconditional.

As we have already seen, faith is a stubborn commitment to God – an unflinching insistence that there is Divine purpose and possibility, even goodness, in the presence of suffering, death and evil – and this commitment transcends the limitations of reason.

Indeed, the Kabbalists explain that faith begins where reason ends.[18] However, one must know rationally and empirically – to the extent that such knowing is possible – when to stop using one's mind and depending on one's reason and simply have faith.

This kind of faith involves the ability to see with one's eyes closed.

Even in our physical world when one wants to see something far away one does not open one's eyes wider, but, to the contrary, one squints – an action which involves nearly closing one's eyes in order to focus better. This is done in order to block out interference which comes from peripheral vision. Also, when one's eyes are open, the field of vision tends to spread out and dissipate at a certain point, whereas when one squints, the power of vision is focused and it is possible to see more clearly. The further away the object, the more one has to squint, the more one has to shut the eye and bring it to a pinpoint.

Ultimately, in a spiritual sense, there is a level of vision which requires the shutting of one's eyes completely.

Spiritual things are very far away indeed, so we have to shut out physical eyes to focus the inner vision of the soul.[19]

Kabbalah's Definition of Soul

All that we have been describing in terms of faith and seeing with one's eyes closed corresponds to a Kabbalistic understanding of the soul and how it functions.

The Kabbalists teach that the human soul has five levels.[20] Metaphorically, we can think of these levels as prisms through which the unified Divine light passes so as to become differentiated and made manifest at various levels of human perception and physical reality. Thus, each prism diminishes the intense strength of Divine light, while accentuating particular properties or potentialities contained in the undifferentiated wholeness of its unity.

The last of these prisms is the fifth and lowest level of soul; it is what allows the five senses and human consciousness to interact with the world.

The next, fourth level, is higher than the previous one; it is what allows us to experience emotions and make them known to others. It allows us to sense people's feelings and interact with them appropriately. It is the level of the heart, the seat of emotionality.

The next prism, the third level of soul, provides us with a sense of boundary between inner and outer, thus provoking a thought process, which in turn enables us to see things with clarity. It is the level of mind, the source of intellect. Being the middle level, it carries special import as it mediates between the two levels below it and the two levels above it.

The next two levels, the second level and the first level are not connected to or dependent on anything physical. They are called "envelopments"[21] because they are beyond the body and are never limited by its constraints. To receive from these "envelopments" we must shut our eyes completely.[22]

These two highest levels of soul are the source of the soul's greatest potential. They represent what is most profound about the image of God at the core of every individual.

Generally speaking, the soul is a kind of receiving set through which understanding and experience of God can be had though we are part of physical existence and are held back by all of its limitations.

All healing – especially self-healing – is ultimately bound up with one's inner sense of being, one's personal intuition of uniqueness, profound mental and emotional potential, and a longing to be whole again with the source of one's origin.

We draw strength from this inner sense of being in times of need. And if we do so successfully, we begin to heal. But what exactly is this fount of intuited strength? No one seems to know precisely. The Kabbalists call it the soul, philosophers refer to it as undifferentiated being.

Before proceeding further in our discussion, let me note that whatever we decide to call it, we are talking about an intuited state of being comprised of latent potentialities undifferentiated in the wholeness of its unity. The difficulty with describing this state of being in more precise terms has to do with the fact that it is absolutely undifferentiated and whole with itself. Thus, any manifestation of it is something other than what it is.

The only way we can discern anything about this state of being is through that aspect of ourselves which is known as the "I." The Kabbalists explain that the "I" is that in ourselves which is at once nurtured by being and which differentiates aspects of that being.[23]

Thus, the "I" can never be captured in its own reflection. I eat, I sleep, I speak, I think, I create, I do all these things, but the sum total of the things I do cannot begin to equal the "I" from which my actions and choices are derived. For the "I" is nurtured directly from my being, which is beyond description.

In other words, the "I" reflects raw power.

This raw power that each one of us possesses is parallel to the power of God. The Kabbalists say that God is HaKol Ya'chol, literally meaning "All Able,"[24]and we who are created in His image are also, to a certain extent, "all able," because God provides us with profound capabilities, making it possible for us to become all that we were meant to become. At their source, these capabilities are part and parcel of our essential being; they are pure potential which remains unified and undifferentiated until it is actualized and articulated in the world through the "I."

This "I" is like the electrical generator of a major city that sends out raw electrical power. Contained within that generator is the potential for every bulb to light and every mix-master or fan or toaster to work, but we don't see bulbs and mix-masters in the generator, we just sense raw power – undifferentiated raw power. As soon as aspects of that raw power are made manifest then they become differentiated, they become the varying degrees of electricity needed to turn on the mix-master and are experienced through the workings of what the mix-master does.

Thus the power of the generator is made manifest through what the mix-master does, just as the power of the "I" is made manifest through what the "self" does.

The "self," in the language of the Kabbalah, is defined a bit differently than it is in the language of modern psychology. My "self" is the perception of who I am, based on what I have done or accomplished in my life.[25]

It is the actualization of the "I." The degree to which I succeed in actualizing the undifferentiated potentialities of my being conveyed through the "I" becomes my sense of "self."

The switching station between the pure potential contained in the "I" and its manifestation as the "self" is will.

What is it that turns on the power in the mix-master of my "self"? My will. Will is that through which the raw power of undifferentiated consciousness is actualized into some form – which might be a thought or an action.

According to the Kabbalists, will is sparked and motivated by the desire that flows from my existential awareness of the unique power and potential inherent in my essential being. It is that awareness which stimulates my will to action – to do the things I do.[26]

But if I were to take all these things I do and put them together, they wouldn't begin, in any way, to actually approach the power of the "I," any more than turning on every appliance in my house could even begin to approach the power of the generator. The "I" is so infinitely more powerful than any possible manifestation of itself that all the manifestations of the "I" combined can't possibly equal the "I." They only reflect its potential.

The Power of Potential

At one point in the Bible, Moses asks to understand God and God responds "Behold, there is a place with me…" The 11th century biblical commentator, Rashi, elaborates on that cryptic phrase by quoting the Jewish oral tradition: "God is the place of the world but the world is not His place."[27]

That is to say, God encompasses the totality of creation, but God is not encompassed, or limited in any way, by creation.

God is responsible for creating and perpetuating the world. God's immanence makes possible all that exists. And yet, if you take all that exists and combine it together, that sum total doesn't begin to equal God. God is in effect telling Moses: "I am the place of the world and yet the world is not my place; I cause the world to exist, and yet I am not held captive or limited in any way by my own creation."

And, therefore, because we are created in the image of God, our potential is also infinitely greater than any manifestation of itself. The totality of our undifferentiated being is infinitely more powerful than any of its possible manifestations.

There are times, of course, when the power of our potential anifests itself in negative ways. We waste energy on things that are not worthwhile; we allow ourselves to be governed by desire and utilize the strength we have in ways that are wrong or inappropriate.

Ultimately, we come to recognize our mistakes but find it difficult to forgive ourselves for what we have done. Our self-image is diminished, and we feel an acute sense of unworthiness, which often leads to hopelessness or despair.[28]

Let us say a man who is suffering physically or emotionally proclaims, "I want to kill myself." If that man really understood what he was saying, the last thing he would do is kill himself.

He is saying, in effect: "The intuitive sense of my undifferentiated potential is so healthy and strong that the 'I' within me wants to kill off those negative aspects of 'self' that keep the 'I' from being manifested correctly." But if he understood that, then he'd know that he could, of course, change his behavior or attitude and manifest the potential that comes through the "I" in a better way.

This also explains why emotional pain hurts.

The pain one feels is out of sync, inconsistent with one's essence, and this is why it is painful. If, however, one's illness becomes consistent with one's essence – for example, when someone terminally ill is nearing death, and there is a kind of internal acquiescence as the body and mind yield to the naturalness of what is happening – then emotional pain ceases to exist.

Which brings us to the question: When do we suffer?

The answer: When we know we should or could be doing better and we're not. When our undifferentiated potential is not being manifested in the world in the way we would like. But that doesn't mean that suicide is the answer. To the contrary, we should be motivated by what we know to find a way of living in the world that better articulates what we implicitly understand to be the greatness of our God-given potential.

That potential does not cease until we draw our last breath. Indeed, some of the most profound things people do and say are in the very last moments of life. Unfortunately, most people don't have a serious understanding of the "I" – of the fact that they are created in the image of God – and therefore they fall into the trap of believing that the "self" and the "I" are the same thing. In other words, they think that "what I do is who I am," or "how much I fail proves that I am no good."

But this is not true. The basis of all repentance – or teshuvah as it is called in Hebrew, meaning "return to God" – is the belief that as long as a person is alive, there is hope. Because any manifestation of the "I" – no matter how negative – can be undone in the next moment by simply manifesting undifferentiated potential in better form. But as soon as I believe that what I've done is absolutely who I am, then, if I have done something truly terrible, there is no aspect of my being worth perpetuating in life.

We can also see this in people's ability or inability to heal. As soon as a patient starts to believe that her body is the ultimate arbiter of her potential for healing, then, if her body is sick enough and she starts to believe that she will die, that is indeed what will happen. But, if she were to realize that the potential for healing is derived from the "I," that this potential is contained in her essential being, then she'd know that the strength of that potential – if channeled correctly – has the ability to overpower and correct any deficiency in her body.

Of course, everybody has to die sometime, and it is possible that this is the time; if so, no matter what the patient does isn't going to reverse the process. But even then, tapping into the "I," accessing the soul, is of benefit, because at the very least, it helps that person die more peacefully.

Having said that, I will continue to insist that there are many instances where, if a person were in touch with the life-force conveyed by the soul, then that person could will himself or herself to health. Indeed, a sick person can access the immortality of the soul via something so deceptively simple as the will to live.

2

The Five Levels of Soul

We will now take a look, in greater detail, at the five levels of soul29 as the Kabbalah understands them. We need to have a clear understanding of this concept because all sickness comes from a breakdown of connection with one or another of these levels. And all healing comes from accessing their power.

The First Level of Soul: Yechidah

The highest level of soul is yechidah, "unity." It is the primordial source of every level of soul manifested beneath itself.

From yechidah comes one's on-going ability to be a catalyst for spiritual experience.

This highest level of soul is not dependent on any aspect of the created universe for its existence. It allows a person to be bound to God steadily and without reason.

From this highest level of soul comes the ability to access the paradox we spoke of previously. For it engenders the power of blind faith, which nothing can take away because it's totally independent of any kind of reason or rationale. It is this highest level of soul, which is the most God-like, that enables us to cling stubbornly through acts of will to a belief in purpose. Very spiritual people can momentarily interact with this level of soul, but are immediately repelled and forced away from its light. The same is true to a slightly lesser extent of chayah, the level of soul just beneath yechidah.

As is known, to enter any rung of spiritual experience requires a surrender of the ego. Thus, the degree of self-abnegation which one is able to attain will determine the richness and profundity of one's experience. The rung of yechidah, however, is unlike any other. To interact with the experience generated by this level of soul requires a total and complete state of self-abnegation. One must separate from self to the point where one is no longer self-aware. That is to say, one is not aware of having had the yechidah experience until one regains one's self-awareness, at which point only the impression of that brief experience remains – like a small child moved away from his mother's embrace remembers only the scent of her perfume having been returned once again to his crib.

Often, adults in terrible crisis will call out "Mommy" or "Daddy," reaching toward their most innate primal sense of security. In that moment, unbeknown to themselves, they are struggling to rise to that level of unity with God associated with yechidah. Intuitively, they are struggling for transcendence, for an experience of wholeness and unencumbered integration.

There is an expression, "There are no atheists in the foxhole." For even atheists will talk in terms of God when they are surrounded by the enemy, bombs are falling and their comrades are being killed; then, out of nowhere comes, "God help me." In so doing, they transcend the immediate in an effort to draw strength from something beyond, where there are no limitations.

This, however, is a reflex reaction, and reflex reactions do not last very long.

Indeed, the average person is really not open to the yechidah level, although in moments of crisis such openness is possible. But that crisis-generated experience won't last because it is merely an escape, dependent on the intensity of the moment. To learn how to deliberately access yechidah takes work and it takes time.

For one to experience yechidah however briefly and be nurtured by its healing potential, one must approach yechidah with a vessel capable of retaining the impression of its light. This vessel is the power of will. That is to say, that if a person moves toward yechidah reflexively as a means of escaping from pain or trauma then that movement is empty of any deliberate sense of self. Whereas, if the attainment of yechidah comes about as a deliberate quest – one that is generated by the will to experience unity beyond the chaos of suffering – then that focused will becomes the vessel for this ultimate experience of the Divine.[30]

The will that takes one up to the highest level of soul called yechidah comes from the level immediately below.

The Second Level of Soul: Chayah

The second level of soul the Kabbalists call chayah, "living essence."

Chayah gives one a subjective sense of identification. It's a sense of one's own uniqueness and undifferentiated potential. And it is this sense of potential and uniqueness that stimulates one's will to continue in life.

The will to act – under the influence of chayah – is evidenced by one's determination to articulate aspects of that uniqueness.

No matter what pressure or suffering is brought to bear on the reality of my existence, still and all I am convinced that if God has seen fit to keep me in life then there are aspects of my remarkable potential that I must nurture and continue to make manifest.

Thus, it is the chayah aspect of soul in each person that nurtures and focuses will in the direction of continued life, accomplishment and productivity. However, this focused will must, at times, move beyond itself to embrace the profundity of faith that emanates from yechidah. In so doing, a renewal takes place. We recognize the depth of our potential with restored clarity of vision, and we experience the confidence necessary to act on what we have seen. Indeed, our "living essence," which is chayah, is re-invigorated and, at times, reborn. Whenever it rises to its source in yechidah and like a child remembering the scent of its mother, it is overcome by feelings of self-assurance and unbridled acceptance.

The Third Level of Soul: Neshamah

The third level of soul is called neshamah.

The Hebrew term neshamah meaning "soul" is related to the Hebrew term neshimah meaning "breathe."

We read in Genesis that God breathed into Adam's nostrils nishmat chayim, "the breath/soul of life."[31]

While another Biblical verse proclaims, "the breath/ soul of the Almighty" gives understanding.[32]

The Kabbalists explain that the neshamah, through breath, gives life to the body and provides the brain with the ability to discern – this then is our ability to process thought, so that we can understand.

Interestingly, the mathematician G. Spencer-Brown, in his book Laws of Form,[33] demonstrates that all thought process is derived from a general sense of distinction between inner and outer. This general sense of distinction can be traced back experientially to the inhaling and exhaling that takes place as we breathe. [We will discuss the role of breath in accessing the soul in Part IV.]

The neshamah is situated between two planes: 1) the faith and will[34] of yechidah and chayah, from which comes the ability to transcend trauma associated with physical limitation, and 2) the realms of emotionality and physical accomplishment which, as we shall see, come from the two lowest levels of soul.

Thus, there are times when aspects of the neshamah at the core of one's mind move upward to become a vessel for the unencumbered will that derives from chayah. This movement is triggered by new information processed by the brain. This happens because the more we learn, the more we realize what there is yet to know. In response to this realization the neshamah reaches beyond itself to the level of chayah in quest of greater focus and will. There it experiences a renewed appreciation of its God-given potential. Then the neshamah rises still further, opening itself in submission so that it can receive from the source of its own origin in yechidah.

The experience of the neshamah as it transcends its rootedness in the mind so that it can receive from chayah and yechidah may be described in the following manner:[35]

The neshamah, inspired by its desire to know beyond what is known, rises to chayah, the place of will. There its strength is reinvigorated as it perceives anew the power of its own potential. From there, it rises still higher, aligning itself with but not grasping the energy of yechidah. In that instant, all consciousness is subdued, overwhelmed by the mystery of faith. All boundaries cease to exist, as the neshamah, in a momentary state of total selflessness, comes in contact with the realm of God's unconditional love.

Then, in the next instant, the neshamah falls away, but it now bears the impression of that momentary encounter. This impression is like an opening, a vacated space, generating a sense of emptiness and void, like that of a child pulled away from its mother's bosom. But, as the neshamah is drawn back down to the level of chayah, it finds itself in possession of an even greater focus of will.

In fact, the emptiness has somehow been transformed into a powerful yearning and thrust of will guided by a sense of something beyond itself. This will is ultimately "unpacked" – differentiated and deciphered – by the mind, which is the seat of the neshamah.

Imagine being lost in the wilderness, in the dead of night. The sky is clouded over and strange sounds fill the air. You are not sure if the sounds are real or not but you are frightened, alone and without a compass. Suddenly, there is a burst of thunder followed by another and you feel totally demolished by the cacophony of sound. Then, almost immediately, the sky is rent by a flash of lightning, stronger and brighter than before. In the illumination of that flash, you catch a momentary glimpse of a beautiful house, somewhere off in the distance. The lightning lasts but a fraction of a second, and you find yourself forced back into darkness. Still, the recollection of that brief experience leaves you with a renewed sense of self. The house has become blurred in your mind, you cannot recall the details of its beauty, yet somehow you have been left with a profound impression of its having been there. As you continue working things out in your mind, you come to know the direction in which you need to walk, stimulated by the beauty you just beheld. You find yourself feeling confident and whole again, ready to engage the future with a renewed lust for life.

Kabbalistically, your already fragile ego lost in the wilderness of confusion and self-doubt was overwhelmed by a thunder-clap of transcendent reality. And you suddenly realized that you are not the ultimate arbiter of your own destiny. This sublimation of ego allows your mind (neshamah) to rise to the level of your unique essence (chayah). At that point, your mind merged with the uniqueness of your essential being, only to experience – in a state beyond conscious awareness – what might be described as a kind of integrated harmony and alignment with your source in God: illuminated by a flash of lightening, a relative but profound sense of coming home.

The neshamah aspect of the soul is the source of one's sense of being – the undifferentiated "I." For as previously explained, the neshamah mediates between the transcendent levels of chayah and yechidah and the lower levels of soul manifested through the body. This being the case, there are aspects of the "I" that are nurtured by undifferentiated potential and therefore the

"I" cannot ever be completely defined in terms of itself. On the other hand, there are aspects of the "I" that are manifested as the "self" through the lower levels of soul, associated with one's physical body, which we shall examine next.

The Fourth Level of Soul: Ruach

The fourth and next to the lowest level of soul, the Kabbalists call ruach. In Hebrew, ruach means "spirit" or "wind" or "direction."

From ruach comes a kind of emotional self-awareness which is brought about by interaction with and comparing oneself to others. (Note that this fourth level of soul is different than the second level of soul, which provides us with a transcendent and totally subjective sense of identity and uniqueness.) Through ruach, we develop our emotional sense of self-awareness based on how we perceive our interactions with others.

In every interaction, there is an angle of perception that determines how we feel about the other person, and ultimately how we feel about ourselves. This angle of perception is sustained through the ruach within us.

Thus, all emotionality is based on ruach. When we have

a healthy relationship to the soul at the level of ruach, we achieve an emotional clarity, unclouded by things that are imagined. But when that connection is warped, our relationships become strained and convoluted. For example, we might read things into a relationship that don't actually exist, or we might accentuate aspects of a conversation that support what we want to believe, rather than listening to the whole of what was said. Indeed, there are lots of pitfalls.

Ruach receives its clarity and balance by becoming a vessel for neshamah. That is to say it must receive into itself the qualities of discernment associated with clarity of mind.

The clarity of neshamah dispensed to ruach, however, is not an ordinary sense of clarity. Rather it is a kind of awareness that includes in itself a sense of ultimate purpose and faith in God.

This being the case, one is able to discern on the level of ruach not only the subjective realities of a given relationship but also the nuances of that relationship as they relate to the direction in which one wants life to proceed. Ultimately, when the level of ruach is perfected, one finds oneself automatically able to integrate what is beneficial from a given relationship while discarding what is not.

The Fifth Level of Soul: Nefesh

The fifth and lowest level of soul, the Kabbalists call nefesh. This name comes from the Hebrew word nafash meaning "rest."

The Kabbalists are telling us that everything we are able to intuit, to know, or to experience emotionally comes to rest within this basic and lowest level of soul.

And it is through the nefesh that we act in the world. For the nefesh enables us to manifest ourselves through the ideas and concrete forms we generate. Thus the sum-total of who we are – our intellect and emotions and identity – is made apparent through our creative acts.

The nefesh corresponds to the senses, which enable us to interact with the whole world. It's how we touch somebody, how we look at one another, what we say, or what we do with our hands – be it playing a musical instrument, or writing, or painting. All these things are made possible by the nefesh. It's that part of the soul that allows us to make manifest what's inside on the outside. It is also the gateway through which experiences of other are internalized.

I was reminded of this recently, when I was invited to give a series of lectures in Montreal. One of the themes I spoke about was joy and self-confidence. At some point during my talk, I presented each person with a sheet of paper and instructed everyone to list their positive traits on one side and their negative traits on the other. Having concluded the exercise, I asked them which had been more difficult – listing the positive or the negative. Everyone agreed that listing the positive had been more difficult. The question then arose: Why?

Most people needed more time to think, but one insightful individual explained that he was very sensitive to his faults, and because they were constantly on his mind, it wasn't difficult to recall them at a moment's notice.

I responded that his answer was quite logical and reasonable, but I didn't think it was entirely truthful. Indeed, in my opinion, it is always easier to list one's negative traits because, in so doing, we are coming up with excuses for why we don't live up to the positive in ourselves.

The key to a balanced nefesh is integrity. What we put into the world cannot be compromised by the need for immediate reward or recognition. We must also safeguard the nefesh against a false sense of security which results from actions and modalities of behavior that are repetitive and predictable. To the contrary, we must constantly open our senses to new experiences and possibilities that deepen our awareness of God and appreciation of life.

3

Connecting with God through the Soul

Now that we understand how the soul functions, we can see more clearly how its various aspects affect healing.

Of course, there are various kinds of healing. When I cut my finger, I put on some iodine and a band-aid, and I don't have to worry about it. But what if I have an illness that has been deemed "incurable"? Then the power of healing that's drawn from the highest place of the soul is necessary.

The more unlikely that medicine has an answer and the more unlikely that any of the standard cures will work, the more necessary it is to go to the highest court for healing.

The highest court is yechidah.

Unfortunately few of us are ever able to access its power.

A terminally ill person, before he finds out his illness is terminal, usually has been sick for a long time. This also means that to some extent his body has become accustomed to illness as well. Such a person, when confronted by the gravity of his situation, is not likely to muster the strength and focus needed to attain this highest level of soul.

He might cry out, "God help me" in a moment of distress. But he is too enmeshed in his suffering to achieve transcendence through this momentary plea. And even if he had been passively in touch with a sense of God all the while, it is unlikely that he will be able to jump-start this condition of passivity and transcend to the level of yechidah.

What needs to take place can happen more readily to a person who has been God-fearing and religious for most of his life. Such people are generally familiar with levels of transcendence and have cultivated ways to access them at will.

But even then the ultimate experience of yechidah is

the most difficult to attain. For it is an experience of total submission and acquiescence to God. So much so that we are not even aware of having undergone the experience until we are forced back and away from it. Only then does consciousness return carrying within itself the impression of having been overwhelmed by yechidah.

In a sense yechidah is that aspect of any experience which is overwhelmingly greater than the sum of its parts.

If you close your eyes and ask yourself, "What was the greatest experience of love I shared with my mother?" then, if you are like most people, you will inevitably see something quite simple. In fact, so simple, that if you were to tell your mother that this image is what represents her profound love, she would probably be very disappointed. And yet, for you, that simple experience engenders a love infinitely greater than the sum of its parts.

When I was a young child, my sister was born. We lived in a three-story building and everyday my mother, carrying my sister in her arms, with me trailing after them, would come out of the building and go down a cement ramp that led to the basement where my sister's carriage was kept. She would put my sister into the carriage and pull it up the ramp onto the street. I would always help her with the pulling. And one day, she turned and said to me, "You know, you're getting stronger all the time." And even now, in moments of weakness I remember my mother telling me, "You're getting stronger all the time."

With that simple sentence my mother connected me with the unlimited potential contained in my yechidah and gave me an unforgettable glimpse of the power sourced at the core of my own being.

Throughout our lives, all of us have had similar experiences that continue to provide strength and healing no matter what our situations happen to be.

An encounter with yechidah is that transcendent aspect of an experience which imprints itself on consciousness in ways that are infinitely more meaningful than the experience itself.

A person trying to heal often feels that her life is falling apart. The security and consistency of everyday living has suddenly become fragmented and unstable. At times

like these, she might want to tap into those aspects
of yechidah that are sources of strength and undying
confirmation. However, she must remember that these
aspects of yechidah – no matter how strength-giving
they may be – are only dim reflections of the real thing.
Ultimately, she must access and allow herself to be
overwhelmed by the tender mercies of God that are part
of every breath she takes.

Ultimately, she must learn to become part of the
mystery of faith, allowing herself to be overcome in
submission to the life force itself.

In God's Image

Generally, one cannot access yechidah without the help
of chayah.

From chayah comes the profound conviction that we
are created in the image of God. And that image must
be cherished and honored for as long as we continue
to breathe. When we are in touch with chayah, we see
ourselves as caretakers of the gift of God's image in
ourselves. We are responsible to nurture that gift and
bring it to fruition to the extent that this is possible

in every deed, in every gesture, and in every show of emotion.

In essence, if we ever experience chayah in the deepest sense, we will always be aware of our own worth and worthiness. And then, even if we momentarily experience loss or are embarrassed by failure, we will never give up hope.

People who are out of tune with chayah may see themselves as insignificant, stupid or useless. For them a serious illness just confirms the fact of their perceived insignificance. People like this will often say, "I see that others live to 70 or 80, and I have cancer at 35, well, I always knew that I was worthless."

Then there are those, who are also out of tune with chayah, who behave in opposite fashion. They see themselves as lord and master of their own lives, the ultimate arbiters of their own destinies. When finally confronted with death, they're stymied, unable to reconcile what is happening to them with what they believed about themselves.

A person who thinks he is god in his own life, and then finds out that he has cancer (which, of course, can only mean that he has been lying to himself all along), such a person gives up on life as soon as it sinks in that he's going to die.

In a sense, a person who sees himself as invincible, full of strength and omnipotent potential, but does not recognize that he is merely a temporary caretaker of a God-given gift, that sort of person has misused chayah and, as a result, has been victimized by what might be termed its "flip side."

But, inevitably, nothing is real that doesn't include a sense of God's presence. And when chayah is appropriately nurtured, we are imbued with a sense of mission in life, and then wonderful things can happen.

The Talmud teaches36 that our mission in life was clearly known to us before we were born. But at the moment of our birth, we were made to forget. Nevertheless, the impression of what we once knew stays with us throughout life. That impression generates a sense of existential emptiness that each of us feels having once known something which we now long to rediscover.

Thus life becomes a quest, each of us looking for

something to fill the void. And when we find any aspect of that something, then we immediately know that it belongs to us since it fits comfortably into our sense of absence.

So basically then, the soul at the level of chayah has the intuitive sense of its own uniqueness which is born from a sense of loss, of absence, of having once understood something and forgotten it, but the impression of having known it is still left. And this impression is the cause of existential will and yearning and desire, and of constant thinking and testing out.

There are moments when we sense aspects of our emptiness filling up. We feel that something profoundly lost has been suddenly returned – that the quest of a lifetime has been vindicated and rewarded. We are like people falling in love at first sight after years of loneliness and relentless searching. The fact that we looked so long adds an extra dimension of pleasure and appreciation to what is finally found.

Existential loneliness and yearning are by-products of the vacated space. This is because the second level of soul chayah (as well as the first level yechidah) is directly derived from the nothingness that existed before creation.[37]

In other words, I want to love God even though it's impossible for me to know God. In the depths of my being I yearn for Him. I yearn for Him because I am created in His image and the very core of my consciousness bears the imprint of His vacated presence.

Deep within myself there is a well-spring of faith and will and a sense of purpose no matter what. This well-spring is chayah which is filled with longing that has no shape, with yearning for God that knows no bounds. The fact that my desire for Him is so limitless and deep confirms that I am worthy. For I bear the imprint of transcendence bestowed upon me by my Creator. Thus I am entitled to pray that He who granted me life should continue to sustain me in life.

Another Chance

When we connect with the level of soul called neshamah during the healing process, then we know beyond any doubt that despite what the outer forms of any disease seem to suggest, or whatever it is that the doctors have to say, ultimately it is within God's power to bring about healing through the infusion of new breath and life sustaining potential.

Giving up is simply not in our spiritual vocabulary. As the Sages thought, "Even if a sharp sword is placed on your neck, don't stop praying for God's compassion."[38]

God is always capable of bringing our hopes for recovery to fruition.

Why do people give up? Usually it is because the habit to give up has been ingrained in them a long time ago.

All of us are born with a sense of yearning connected to the level of soul called chayah as explained previously.

On the level of the neshamah (the undifferentiated "I"), this yearning is translated into a set of ideals. This is why so often in their youth people are highly idealistic and filled with a mission to change the world and make it a better place. But, as time goes on, they lose track of their ideals. The once powerful sense of their essential being grows dim.

It doesn't happen overnight; people give up their ideals little by little. They become preoccupied by trying to earn a living and achieve social status, by raising a family, or by other life concerns, and their ideals simply become overshadowed by their everyday needs and worries. Regular, normal, everyday things take up all their physical, mental and emotional energy.

But the more people give up on their ideals the more they live a life out of sync with the neshamah. Still, the neshamah continues to yearn to fulfill its mission as a vehicle for God's goodness. Even when suppressed, it constantly cries out to be heard, but the demands of everyday life cause most folks to turn a deaf ear to its calling.

If that happens to you, as you get older you will almost certainly find yourself visited by a sense of discouragement or fatigue. And sooner or later, you are brought back to a confrontation with the neshamah. You will come to realize that your life has become repetitive and predictable, empty of meaning and true satisfaction. You will come to realize that too much of your life has become focused on things that should have only helped you fulfill your ideals but instead took center stage.

This realization is what is called "the mid-life crisis." Because of it, people at mid-life change careers, learn to play musical instruments, devote time to charitable causes. This is because this confrontation with the neshamah reminded them of their aspirations and, this time around, they did not squelch the feeling.

Not to respond to the neshamah is to invite illness, for whatever is suppressed ultimately festers.

This gnawing realization that who you are is far short of who you might have been will sooner or later make you sick. Illness is a manifestation of limitation. When you are subconsciously or consciously frustrated, that frustration is going to manifest itself in the body as some kind of illness.

But in the spiritual world of unlimited potential, it is never too late. When you get in touch with the neshamah, you come back to your higher self – the higher aspects of your "I." You then bring a sense of that higher self to bear on your everyday life, and with it, you bring healing.

If you keep focused on your ideals, then your whole mental and emotional and physical being will infuse that aspiration. And if you believe that you are capable of something (assuming you are rational), then you can make it happen. Of course, not in the same way if you had never abandoned your ideals in the first place, but you will get a second chance.

How is that possible?

Through God's mercy.

I have a theory that this is the message of déjà vu – the feeling that you've been there before, when you're in a certain place and something happens that's profoundly familiar and yet, try as you might, you can't recall ever having been there or done that before. But still, you could swear that this is a replay of a past event.

I believe that the message of déjà vu is that opportunity does indeed knock more than once, but it doesn't always present itself in the same package. There is a certain kind of dynamic, a certain kind of rhythm that pulsates with meaning that you were supposed to connect with in the past. But you didn't, and so, many years go by and you are again placed in a situation which intrinsically holds the same possibility, but packaged differently. This produces the feeling of déjà vu.

Déjà vu can be understood as God giving you another chance to recapture the essential ingredients contained in opportunities gone by, because you missed out the first time. If you can be sensitive to the movement, to the rhythm, to the impulse the second time although it appears in a different form, and if you can manage to take advantage of that inherent potential, then you will have achieved atonement and healing.

But take note – not every illness was meant to be healed. After all, sometimes it is true that your time has simply come. But healing, atonement and/or peace can be yours as long as there is life and consciousness – the secret is to provide your essence with new form. (In other words, start by improving yourself and see what happens.)

Feeling and Knowing

When we connect with the level of soul called ruach, which is the seat of our emotions, we are able to integrate what we know about our mission in life with how we feel.

Unfortunately, too often people get waylaid. They get emotionally involved with things and people, and expend their energies in ways that are not integrated with the ideals they always wanted to live by. This happens because, while they know what they should do, their feelings and desires pull them in different directions.

So, for example, a person who smokes has, without a doubt, been told any number of times that smoking is dangerous to health and linked to many different types of disease. However, knowing this, she continues to smoke anyway, because it gives her pleasure and she finds this pleasure emotionally gratifying. And this emotional gratification overshadows any feeling of fear that she might otherwise have for her health. Thus, her knowledge is not integrated with her emotions.

Behaving this way in various areas of life, obviously invites trouble.

Another example of this sort of thing is a love relationship gone sour. It can happen because we allow relatively petty emotional differences to stand in the way of what otherwise could have been a truly gratifying relationship. And it can happen because fantasy overwhelms reality – as when we read into a relationship what is not there – and a relationship that is obviously not satisfying is maintained despite what it is missing. In either instance, one's mind and heart are not in sync.

Illness is but one painful manifestation of this lack of integration.

The only repair is putting our emotions in line with what we know is best for us. When we do that we connect to ruach.

A connection with ruach means aligning our emotions with our intellect, which is the only way to wholeheartedly pursue the best course in life. Thus ruach, which is spirit or emotion, also means direction. That is to say, emotions should be directed or guided by the intellect.

Another factor worth mentioning when discussing the lack of synchronicity between intellect and emotions, mind and heart, is the inability to maintain a sense of inspiration. Often we get excited about an idea or an ideal but lack the enthusiasm to carry through. It's difficult to nurture the best in ourselves to fruition. We have to learn how to love what we know is best for us in a way similar to a pregnant woman who does everything possible to take care of her body and physical well-being, while waiting in anxious anticipation to bring the baby to term. We, too, must fall in love with that in ourselves which hasn't yet been born into form, nurture it and make it our greatest passion.

Expressing the Soul through the Senses

At the lowest level of nefesh, which is connected to the senses, we make manifest what's inside on the outside.

Where does this go wrong?

A good example is an artist who has found a unique way of expressing himself, and because his expression is so original, the general public is not likely to be accustomed to that modality of expression. So this artist will at first (perhaps for the duration of his lifetime) go unrecognized. Until his unique style is acknowledged, he may have to earn a living doing something mundane, and may even betray his gift on occasion by imitating the painting style of others rather than expressing his own unique soul.

Whatever gifts we have been given – and that includes talents, skills, as well as the limbs and organs that bring them to fruition – were meant to portray what is unique about us in the world.

As long as our bodies help us to express ourselves with integrity, then they have a purpose and we live. But when we begin to feel that who we are in the deepest sense can no longer be manifest through the bodies that we have, then our bodies begin to close down to an even greater extent.

So, for example, we notice that, as a rule, older people begin to lose touch with their senses. Their sense of smell and taste diminish; their eyes fail; they are not as easily aroused sexually. Their senses become dulled. Likewise, they lose energy, are less excited about initiating creative projects. It's as if these people are shutting down their nefesh.

But others, equally as old, remain vital and alive. They continue to love life, they don't permit a shutdown. They demonstrate to others that there is a certain innate health and healing in the sheer sense of being alive. Such people have managed to perfect the nefesh so that it continues to convey a lust for life from levels of soul beyond itself.

Ultimately, we have to create space between ourselves and whatever it is that we are experiencing. If we believe that we and what is happening to us are one and the same, then it becomes impossible to analyze our situation from a point of balanced perspective.

If we are suffering and are overwhelmed by our suffering, then there is no way out. Similarly, if we are prospering, and we come to identify with our prosperity, then the moment we cease to prosper, it's as though we were totally destroyed.

Therefore, it is important for all of us to be aware of context, to always have a sense of perspective that enables us to maintain this distinction between who we are and what is happening to us.

What is happening to us often seems concrete and absolute – like words brought together in a sentence that has but one meaning. But, in essence, words are nothing more than groupings of letters, which when undone, can create new words that hold still greater meaning.

Thus, each of us is really a soul in the midst of prayer, constantly struggling to fashion something new from past experiences, from words already spoken. Only God is absolute.

4

Visualization Exercise for Part Three

Close your eyes, relax and breathe out three times.

You are standing in front of a ladder, which is firmly balanced on the ground. Its head extends into the very heavens.

Climb the ladder one step at a time moving toward its highest rung. If you like, you can take off articles of clothing along the way to make your climbing easier. Drop whatever clothes you remove to the ground and continue to climb until you are standing balanced on the highest rung.

Breathe out.

When you reach the top rung of the ladder, see the

heavens open to reveal the Light of Constant Renewal.

See and know that light as it descends, gently unfolding and embracing the whole of your body until you are completely enveloped in a cocoon of new beginning.

Breathe out.

Breathe in the light that surrounds you, causing it to merge with the portion of God's light at the essential core of your being.

See and feel your Godly essence being strengthened and rejuvenated.

Breathe out.

Breathe the light of your rejuvenated essence into those places inside yourself that are still dark and in pain. Exhale the darkness and watch it leave you like black smoke which floats away and disappears beyond the horizon. When those places of darkness are filled with light, continue to breathe the light of your Godly essence into the rest of your body. Exhale any darkness you may encounter, until your whole body is filled with light.

Breathe out.

Begin to descend the ladder, slowly, one step at a time. When you reach the ground, see the clothes lying near the ladder. Decide which of these clothes you want to wear again. Put them on, and burn the rest. Then bury the ashes.

Breathe out and open your eyes.

PART FOUR

ACCESSING THE ESSENCE OF LIFE

1

Origins of Life

How precious is a sigh ... for a sigh is the completion of what is lacking.

Through breath, which is the spirit of life, the entire universe was created. As it says in the Book of Psalms, "By the word of God the heavens were created, and by the breath of His mouth all of their hosts."[39]

And the renewal of creation of the whole world will also be through the concept of breath as is written, "When You send forth Your spirit, they will be created, and You will renew the face of the earth."[40]

... The life of humankind is breath. As is written in Genesis, "And God breathed into the nostrils of Adam the

soul of life."[41]

The Sages clearly state: If breath stops, life stops. So it is apparent that the life of all things has to do with spirit or breath. And, therefore, if there is anything lacking in a particular thing, it is always connected to the life, the spirit, or breath in that particular thing. For it's always the breath that sustains. And the sigh is a long breath.

When a person takes a long breath - in other words when a person sighs about what he is lacking - then he draws the breath of life to the place of lack ... Through sighing one makes whole whatever was lacking.

Adapted from the teachings of
Rebbe Nachman of Breslov[42]

In order to appreciate these words of the great 18th century Hassidic Master, Rebbe Nachman of Breslov, we have to understand that God, according to the Bible, created the universe through the power of speech:

> And God said, "Let there be light" and there was light ... And God said, "Let the earth give forth its produce" ... and so it did ... and God said "Let the waters swarm with living creatures ..."[43]

God spoke the universe into existence.

But if we look carefully at the whole biblical account of creation, we find that God spoke all of creation into existence, except for one thing. When it came to creating the human being, as the Bible relates it, God didn't repeat the standard litany: "Let there be man, and there was man." Instead, God breathed life into the nostrils of a form that He created from the dust of the earth. And when He did so, that lump of clay became a living human being. Therefore, God did not speak the human being into life, He breathed the human being into life.

It is an astounding realization. Everything in the whole universe is a manifestation of speech, but the soul of humankind is a manifestation of breath.

The Zohar, the chief work of the Kabbalah, goes so far as to suggest that when God breathed into Adam, He breathed from Himself.[44]

The Zohar is using a metaphor, of course, but it is making the point that the essence of the human condition is as close as one can possibly get to God Himself. We are, in truth, all created in the image of

God. We live by the very breath of God.

Between Speech and Breath

There is a hierarchy between breath and speech. For one thing, we all realize that it's not possible to speak without breathing, but it is possible to breathe without speaking. In other words, breath is more primal than speech. In fact, breath is what gives life and possibility to the world – it is the soul of the word through which the world was created.

Adam and Eve were created last in the order of creation, and according to the Sages,[45] the reason they were created last was so they could, in one way or another, elevate all creation back to its source in God. They were supposed to see beyond physical form – which is a manifestation of God's word – and raise that form to its source in breath. Therefore, there is nothing in creation more powerful than humankind.

This explains a difficulty that the famed 11th century biblical commentator Rashi and many others have had with the verse in Exodus, which reads: "In six days God created the heavens and the earth, and on the seventh day He ceased from work, and He rested."[46]

Rashi points out that the Hebrew word vayinefash doesn't really mean "and He rested." Literally it means, "and He breathed." He goes on to explain that what happened here is that God stopped working, so to speak, to "catch His breath."

Kabbalistically, however, this is understood to mean that in six days God created everything through speech and, on the seventh day, He went back to breathing without speaking.

From that point on, all of the forms that came into being as a result of God's speech have been sustained by God's breath. And so, continuation of life is dependent upon God's breath.

As long as we are in touch with our breath, we need not have any fear – our physical self, through breath, is connected to God.

Rebbe Nachman once said that all evil in the world can be traced back to two initial causes – either we love what we shouldn't love, or we are afraid of what we need not fear.[47]

And when we talk about things we love that shouldn't be loved, or things that we fear that we shouldn't really be afraid of, we're always talking about things that occupy space, things that have form.

If you are suddenly brought into confrontation with some terrifying form (or notion, or concept, which are also types of form) what's your immediate reaction? You stop breathing. This is because form – when seen as something terrifying and absolute – stifles the fluidity and continuity of breath.

If a person falls into a state of panic, what do the doctors tell her to do immediately? Breathe. And if she takes long breaths, she calms down. Implicit in the human condition is the instinct for preservation, for reconnection to life – and that is breath. Breath is more primal than anything else in existence, no matter how important or how threatening it may seem.

The Primacy of Breath

From the moment of birth, we breathe.

A little child comes into the world and begins to breathe, then he grows up a little bit, and he begins to learn. One of the formal things he is likely to learn early on is the alphabet. And the alphabet has a lot to do with form and breath.

It's easy to see in the Hebrew alphabet – which many believe is the foundation of all alphabets – because the vowels are actually written differently than the consonants. The consonants are the actual letters; the vowels are not written as letters in their own right, but as dots and dashes under the consonants.

In order to pronounce or understand the meaning of any word, one has to know which vowels to vocalize in conjunction with the letters that make-up a particular word.

Thus in the Hebrew language, letter combinations are given meaning and expression through the vowels that are joined to them. And this is why the Kabbalists teach that the letters are like bodies and the vowels are like souls.48

As a child begins to speak, we teach him the letters and the vowels needed to pronounce them. When he reaches the age of five or six, he no longer pays attention to the letters or to the sounds – those things are taken for granted. After a while, the child is able to read. In time, he can pick up a book and enjoy its concepts.

As learning progresses, the child is told that what really

matters are concepts. And concepts are ultimately confirmed when they are manifested in form. But form is only meaningful in a physical reality.

That is how we all grow up. And in so doing we become overly attached to concepts and forms. We forget that our ability to perceive concepts is rooted in breath, which first manifests as sounds that become vowels which give life to the letters that become the words through which concepts are expressed. Ultimately we fall in love with absolutes – or the perceived absolutes of concept and form – forgetting their origins in breath.

This forgetfulness is a shame, because it cuts us off from something primal – a basic appreciation of the life force.

And so it's a shame that we lose that awareness, because it connects us with something primal – with a basic understanding of life's processes.

So for example, if your best friend asked you to describe to her your greatest pain or your deepest fear, assuming you were willing to do that, you could only tell her what you consciously understand about the pain, or that fear. But the pain or the fear is often rooted in things that are much, much more profound and deeper than anything that can be described by language, so after a while, you would realize that you only managed to communicate a superficial meaning. But suppose your best friend asked you, instead, to tell her how your pain or your fear "sounds"? Then you would be able to utter that which can't be spoken. The sound you would make from deep within you would communicate so much more than anything that could have been spoken in words. And behind that sound is the power of breath.

As noted earlier the word for breath in Hebrew is closely related to the word for soul, and it describes the middle level of soul called neshamah. The neshamah interfaces between the highest levels of soul, those not connected to the physical, and the lowest levels of soul, those that interact with the physical. It does so through breath, as we shall soon see.

Simply put, the soul of the human being is manifest first and foremost in breath, and it is articulated in sound.

2

The Power of Breath and Sound

When people decide they don't want to breathe anymore, it means they don't have the will to continue in life.

As long as we have the will to live, breathing is automatic, it's unconscious, we don't have to want to do it in order for it to get done. It just happens. It's as automatic as the instinct for survival.

Will, survival, life, they're all the same thing. They're all rooted in the soul, which provides life through breath.

Indeed, every state of the human condition is reflected in breath. No matter what we are experiencing emotionally or physically, that experience is reflected in breath. Our breathing actually changes according to what we are feeling. At those moments when we get in touch with breath, we're making a statement – that we are attached to the will to continue.

Of course, this too is automatic; we don't even have to be consciously aware of this process to make the statement. But holding on to the will to continue is more powerful than any concept confronting us that tells us the end is close. It is more powerful, because concepts are rooted in language, but breath is rooted in life, in God.

Therefore when we breathe, we take into ourselves from outside. We take into ourselves from places of transcendence and give life to the places of absence.

Thus, Rebbe Nachman says that when a person sighs – and a sigh is an intake of breath – he makes whole whatever was lacking.

Levels of Breath

Levels of breath are parallel to levels of consciousness/ soul.

In the last section we talked about the five levels of

the soul. The highest level of soul we described was yechidah, which means "unity," and which imbues one with the potential to live life as a constant catalyst for spiritual experience. From yechidah comes the higher will that manifests in one's existential yearning for transcendence. It is the kind of will that enables a person to cling stubbornly to God with faith and innocence. It is this highest level of soul that we need to tap into when we feel overwhelmed by chaos, or illness, or tragedy.

Rebbe Nachman of Breslov taught: "It is the way of Satan to magnify misfortune."[49] Perhaps another way of putting it might be: "Depression is the interest we pay to misfortune."

If we are in the throes of despair, if we are on the brink of total hopelessness, if we are one with our woe and there's nothing we can think about in the future, nor anything from our past that gives us the courage to continue in life, how can we attach ourselves to that experience of will that renews our faith and our ability to heal?

In the last section, I discussed how the experience of the highest level of soul, yechidah, "unity," is attained through chayah, the level of soul just beneath it.

Chayah, "living essence," is the source of one's sense of being created in the image of God.

When chayah is accessed, we experience anew the uniqueness of our innermost essence and the vastness of its undifferentiated potential. In that same instant, we also realize how little of that potential has been brought to fruition and how much of our uniqueness has gone unnoticed. We are overcome by a sense of humility and great longing, causing our chayah to rise to the level of yechidah. There, it is momentarily overwhelmed and impressed upon by the mystery of faith, like a child held tightly in its mother's bosom, from which all healing is derived. In that moment, the child and the security it is experiencing are integrated and bound together in undivided unity.

Chayah is not accessed through either sound or words. It is stimulated through a focus of breath from the third level of soul, the neshamah. The neshamah as we previously explained means "breath" or "soul." It mediates between the "envelopments" of chayah and yechidah and the lower levels of soul, ruach and nefesh. This mediation depends on breath and its eventual manifestation through sound and words. The manifestation of breath necessary to reach chayah Rebbe Nachman calls the "silent scream."[50]

Rebbe Nachman explains that this silent scream is so powerful that it can cause the very heavens to tremble and yet someone sitting next to the person who is screaming doesn't hear a thing.

The silent scream is a focus of breath through the lungs, and out of the mouth. It's the kind of breath that comes from the life-force deep within us, beyond form or pain or ordinary reason.

The silent scream connects us to chayah and opens us to the experience of yechidah to the extent that we merit it – at any time when we're so overcome we can't speak, we can't sing, we can't even scream out loud. When all we want to do is lie in bed in the fetal position, the one option that's always available is the silent scream – a focus of breath through which we might momentarily touch the level of yechidah, the first expression of primordial will, the source of faith and all-encompassing unity.

The energy of yechidah is sourced in the Divine nothingness or Divine altruism that allows for creation.

It exists totally independent of physical cause and effect, reason, or even sound. Thus, it's the silent scream that opens us to its potential.

Sound and the Levels of Soul

It is well known that no two people have the same fingerprints, but it is less well known that no two people have the same voiceprints. When voices are electronically recorded and a graphic representation is made, we see that any given utterance is uniquely characteristic of the individual speaker.

No two people have the same voice, and the sound they make carries with it the imprint of each one's uniqueness.

Voice, of course, is regulated by the body, which is why the three lower levels of soul connected to the physical are accessed through an actual sound.

The level of neshamah itself is accessed through a loud scream repeated slowly over and again, which eventually gives way to a melody without words, sung quietly and with great intensity.[51]

We said earlier that from neshamah comes the ability

to discern, to know inner from outer on a subjective level. In order to compose a melody there's got to be discernment. It may be a subjective, unconscious kind of automatic discernment, but it's discernment nonetheless. For music depends on the tonal scale and, in composing a melody, one chooses to take this note over that note, and that's discernment. And so when one compiles a set of notes and puts them together in order to compose a melody, one engages in selectivity.

Often melodies are created experientially in the unconscious mind. By singing melodies particularly those of one's own creation, we refine our relationship to the neshamah, thus achieving greater levels of clarity and perception. Melodies strengthen or create harmony in ourselves as we sing them, allowing us to confront situations of chaos from a perspective of clarity.

Then we come to the level of ruach. Ruach means "spirit" or "direction," and it is the seat of emotionality. As explained earlier, ruach has to do with awareness derived from relating to, and comparing one's self with, others.

This kind of awareness inevitably produces a state of emotional disposition which tends to be highly charged, often out of balance and chaotic, sometimes depressed, occasionally pleasing in ways that don't last, and always overwhelmingly subjective. In short, the level of ruach, from which emotions derive, doesn't stand a chance as a conduit for healing or emotional fortitude unless it is influenced by the kind of clarity associated with one's neshamah and its melody without words. This clarity, when it is drawn down to the realm of ruach, becomes a melody with words. This clarity is further enhanced when a person sings a song for which he or she composed the lyrics and melody.

Often the ideals we aspire to in our thoughts are more harmonious than the fragmented experiences that trouble our hearts. Putting words to our melodies, therefore, refines the level of ruach. Shards of broken vessels are brought together and relationships are repaired when guided by a melody that engenders a sense of order beyond ourselves.

Finally, we get to the lowest level of soul called the nefesh. Nefesh is that aspect of our soul that acts in the world. For the most part, our instincts come from the nefesh. Even an animal has a spark of nefesh.[52]

For a human being, nefesh is accessed by regular speech

– by the ability to express oneself to God and others as precisely as possible.

All levels of soul come to rest and are manifested through nefesh. Indeed, what we feel and what we know – and that which we aspire to align with our focus of will and our strength of faith – are all made known in the world through our speech. We speak not only in words, but through our actions and deeds as well. Nevertheless, our ability to explain ourselves clearly, through the spoken word, is the key needed to refine the level of nefesh.

The process we've been describing is a natural and dynamic movement. Will, which is sourced in the highest levels of soul, is reflected in breath and can be accessed through breathing with conscious focus and intent. Indeed, the silent scream is a primal revelation of will. The lower levels of soul, which are aligned with our physical selves, are stimulated through sound – an audible scream, melody without words, melody with words, and regular speech spoken as precisely as possible. Such speech puts us at ease, clears the mind and allows us to focus. Once liberated from false fears, illusion and negative self-perception, we find that our words begin to flow. Without effort we are able to feel and speak that which, just moments ago, was deemed inexpressible. And, along with this uninhibited stream of consciousness, comes new insightfulness, which is a necessary prerequisite in the ongoing pursuit of healing methodology.

It's important to note that not everybody has to start in the beginning of this process. In fact, for some people it might not be advisable to start in the beginning. After all, you don't take drugs for your heart if you don't have heart disease. The idea is that you get a sense where clarity is necessary in your life, where the healing is necessary in your life, where resolution has to take place, where something has to open in order to create the space for the healing to take hold.

But there are people who really are at their wits' end, who are at the brink of despair. For them the silent scream is the answer. However, there are many people who are not anywhere near the brink of despair, so there's no reason for the silent scream. Maybe what they need is a little more clarity. Maybe what they have to do is sing —a melody without words or with words, or maybe they simply have to speak. It's really hard to diagnose, especially in another person, where one needs to begin.

You could, in a superficial way, experiment. If you want to connect to some healing energy, perhaps you need to talk about it with God, or with your best friend, or with your mother, or father, or doctor. If that doesn't work, then maybe what you need to do is sing. Maybe you don't feel like singing songs that have words, so you sing songs that don't have words. And when that's just not enough, there's always the silent scream.

To play with these levels of sound and understand their connection to different levels of soul is to develop for oneself a dynamic of healing – the ability to access appropriate levels of healing energy depending on one's state of mind or physical condition.

The main thing is not to despair. Yes, it takes a while for the ordinary person to learn to access levels of transcendence, but practice makes perfect. And nothing worthwhile comes easily. Trusting in our God-given potential is sometimes more difficult than trusting in God. Still, if God has chosen to keep us in life, then there must be something positive that we are yet meant to accomplish. Find that thing, no matter how seemingly insignificant, and act on it. Remember that a little light can dispel much darkness.

Once Rabbi Yisrael Salanter, the 19th century founder of the Mussar Movement, was on his way home having spent his day in the house of study. It was well after dark, when passing a shoemaker's shop, he remembered that his shoes were in need of repair. Entering the shop he took off his shoes and was about to hand them to the shoemaker when he noticed that the candle the man was using for light was about to go out. Knowing that candles were expensive and that people in business usually limited themselves to one candle a day, Rabbi Salanter apologized for coming so late and began to put his shoes back on. But the shoemaker looked up from what he was doing and said, "Don't worry, as long as the little candle is burning, we can fix everything in need of repair."

From that day on, Rabbi Salanter was often heard repeating the shoemaker's words, "As long as the little candle is burning we can fix everything in need of repair." For the soul of man is a like a flickering candle and as long as there is life everything can be repaired.

And this we read in the Book of Proverbs: "The soul of

man is the candle of God."[53]

3

The Sound of Thunder

Joy is primarily in the heart, as is written,[54] *"you have given joy into my heart." But it is impossible for the heart to rejoice until one first rids the heart of its crookedness, so that he might have a straight heart. Only then can the heart experience joy, as is written,*[55]

"To those who are straight of heart, there is joy." And the way we get rid of the heart's crookedness is through thunder.

Adapted from the teachings of
Rebbe Nachman of Breslov[56]

Perhaps the "crookedness of the heart" that Rebbe Nachman is referring to has to do with one's attachment to form. It's when the heart loves what it shouldn't love or fears what it shouldn't fear. It's when the heart pulsates in a way that's out of sync with a sense of purpose, with a sense of God, with a sense of one's own uniqueness. For, after all, each person is created in the image of God.

In order to straighten out the heart, one needs the concept of "thunder." As the Talmud states, "Thunder was only created in order to get rid of the crookedness of the heart."[57]

If you are ever out in the middle of a storm, and suddenly you hear thunder, your heart is bound to leap. But what is thunder in the subjective world of the human condition?

It's the voice that a person brings out of his mouth during the time of his prayer. And from this voice, expressed with power and passion, comes thunder. For it is written in the Zohar: "When the voice goes forth and hits up against the rain clouds then a sound is transmitted to creation and that sound is thunder."[58]

Rebbe Nachman explains the meaning of that passage from the Zohar as follows: The concept of thunder has to do with power. When a person puts forth his voice in prayer with great power, the very power of his voice hits like thunder against the rain clouds."

And what are the rain clouds that the Zohar is talking about? Consciousness. For from consciousness rains down new revelatory understanding, drop by drop.

As the Zohar[59] interprets the verse from The Song of Songs, "A well of living water drops down from Lebanon."[60]

This word Lebanon shares a common Hebrew root with the word libuna, which means "whiteness." Explains the Zohar, "There is a well of living water that drops down from Lebanon, from the white substance of the brain. When the sound of one's voice is emitted with power in prayer, it hits up against these rain clouds of consciousness. Then a sound is heard in creation and that sound is called thunder."

When the sound of one's prayer comes out of a person's mouth with great force, it hits up against the rain clouds of consciousness and explodes in one's head like thunder. And this thunder is transmitted to creation, that is to say it is transmitted to the heart, which inspires creation, and straightens out the crookedness of the heart.

It is important to remember that there is the spoken word, and the voice upon which this word is carried. The voice, the intonation, is much more profound than what's being said.

Let's take an example of two people, both of whom are raising funds for the same charity. Both approach the same wealthy man and ask him for money. To one of them he gives a $1,000, and to the other he says, "All right, here's $20, go away." When the two collectors compare what happened, they realize that they both said the same thing to the same person, so why did he give one so much more money than the other? Were he to be asked why, the wealthy man would undoubtedly respond, "Because I liked the way he asked."

It's not what we say, it's how we say it. It's the intonation of our voice.

And so there are words that are uttered in prayer, but they are not uttered with passion, with strength, with a revelation of inner aspiration. They're just spoken. But the sound of the voice expressed with power and passion – not the words, the voice – is what hits up against the rain clouds of consciousness.

Consciousness is like rain clouds; it contains, in undifferentiated form, all potential, which has to be stimulated and aroused.

What does it take to make me see something different, from a different point of view? The power of my own voice exploding like thunder in my head. It is heard and felt, its vibrations straighten out my heart.

And as it does that, the clouds break, so to speak, and drop by drop, I experience a new awareness.

When consciousness is stimulated, new awareness is brought into existence, and with that comes a change of heart, a greater focus on what's truly consistent with the wholeness of my being, of creation as it reflects God. And yet, the sound of voice – emitted in prayer with strength – is not always the same.

For some, it might be the silent scream or the audible scream; for others, it might be a melody – a melody without words, or with words; for still others, it might be the ability to clearly and efficiently articulate what needs to be said in ordinary words.

But whatever that sound is – and for different people
at different times it's different kinds of sound – if
it hits up against the rain clouds of consciousness
like a thunderclap and is experienced in the heart, it
effectively changes us in terms of how we live and what
we consider to be important. And, at the same time, it
enlightens us, rains down into our sense of things a new
understanding, new clarity and healing.

4

Visualization Exercise for Part Four

Breathe out three times.

See and know the essence of yourself that is in the image of God.

Breathe out.

Look into your skull and see the rain cloud that holds in itself potential healing and greater awareness.

Breathe out.

From that essence in yourself which is in the image God, scream the silent scream with all your might – scream again and again, silently with focus and power.

Scream until the cloud is pierced.

Hear the thunder as the cloud bursts – feel and know its reverberations, straightening the crookedness of your heart.

Breathe out.

Experience the raindrops of healing and greater awareness, reviving and comforting.

Breathe out and open your eyes.

CONCLUSION
A Transcendent Melody

A woman came to me for help. She had a loving and devoted husband and four beautiful children. Her last child, however, had been stillborn. Haunted by the experience, she was depressed and found it difficult to sleep. After several sessions, she mentioned that, while pregnant with each of her children, she would compose a melody with that child in mind, and each day, she would hum or sing it until the child was born. I asked her to share with me the melody she had composed for her last child, the one who was stillborn. She obliged. To my ear, her composition was filled with love, longing and expectation.

I then gave her a breathing exercise to help her relax. I asked her to close her eyes and sing this melody over and over while seeing the unborn child in her womb. She told me that the child seemed happy and content and radiated a kind of glow at the sound of her voice. I encouraged her to communicate with the child in her mind while continuing to sing.

As she later related to me, the child told her how

grateful he was for the warmth and security conveyed to him by her song. Gathering her courage, she asked him why his life had ended before he was born. He responded saying, "I really don't know. All I can say is that it needed to happen." And then she asked, "But why me? Why was I chosen to mourn for a child I never knew?" He replied, "I'm sorry I was the reason for your suffering. But you were strong and were able to comfort me at this stage of my journey."

She continued to observe the child in her mind's eye as it lifelessly left her body and was buried in a cemetery not far from her home. Through it all, she remained bound to her melody, which she continued to sing over and over.

After a time she fell silent and realized that a fresh insight had found its way to the tip of her tongue. She turned to me and said, "Wherever we journey, we journey toward ourselves. And sometimes people's paths intersect along the way. Then, for a short time, they travel together." She returned home in peace.

How good it is to discover our melody, to sing our own song – to sort out and bring together in harmony those wordless sounds that give expression to the motivations and desires that inspire our every gesture, word and deed. The sound of our voice reflects all that we are and much of what we may yet become. But that sound must be refined. Together with whatever else it may contain, it must be heard in terms of itself. That is to say, it must directly reflect the life force and breath in which it is sourced.

Our melody must be immanent and transcendent, embracing both heaven and earth. It must not be overwhelmed by outside forces or become a mere echo of what was or is. Rather, like breath itself, our melody must animate all that we are, while moving toward what we might yet become.

Every melody is a combination of sounds, each of which is an expression of breath that has never been breathed. Thus, our melody steadfastly binds us to life as we continue to sing. And if, as our melody issues forth from our lips, we choose to contemplate things of the past, a new and refreshing perspective will inevitably surface and make itself known.

Just let go and allow your life's journey to continue.

APPENDIX
The Mystical Understanding
of the Life Force

How we experience the dynamics of sacred space in terms of sickness and healing is dependent, to a large extent, on how we relate to the fundamental life force – a life-force that is both hidden and revealed, removed from us and accessible at one and the same time. The very fact of its paradoxical nature, according to the Kabbalists, is what allows for the sacred space in which healing can take place.

If you are interested in understanding how this works and are willing to engage with the intricacies of Kabbalistic thought, then you might want to read this section carefully, perhaps more than once. Hopefully, you will become sensitive to the profound structure being described. Don't struggle overly much with each detail but rather try to experience its poetic movement. In time why this exercise in mental and emotional gymnastics is necessary for a mystical Kabbalistic understanding of healing should become clear.

The Mystery of Vacated Space

Sacred space is the space within us which contains unlimited potential for many things, among them healing. We understand that for us to be able to access that sacred space we must remove whatever blocks us and connect with the source of sacred space – "vacated space."

Vacated space is the mystical concept, which forms the context needed for creation. It is the beginning of all beginnings – that which allows for creation and the ongoing manifestation of new possibilities of which healing is but one.

In examining the Kabbalistic model of creation, we must remember that mystics, of necessity, use the language of metaphor. As they tell it, it all began because God wanted to create the universe. He didn't have to create the universe, He was not missing anything, He was not going to become more perfect or more whole in so doing. By definition God needs nothing – He is absolutely unified and harmonious and therefore anything he does is altruistic.[61]

Thus, the mystics teach that God created the world to

give of His good to His creation.[62]

But where did God put the universe? There was no room for the universe, since all that existed was God. Therefore, God created the necessary space. He did so by constricting the light of His infinite essence, or, put another way, by constricting His will, which emanates from His essence.[63]

God's essence was not changed in so doing. God remained God. But God's will was withdrawn and limited, so to speak, to make room for His creation.[64]

To understand the difference between essence and will in more familiar terms, imagine for a moment that you wake up in the morning and the first thing you want is a cup of coffee. So you put the pot of coffee on the stove, and you get a cup, spoon and saucer, sugar, milk, whatever you need for your perfect cup of coffee. You are tapping your fingers waiting for that coffee to percolate, and finally it is ready. You pick up the pot ready to pour, anticipating the pleasure of drinking it … and just then the phone rings. On the phone is your best friend who says, "Listen, there's an emergency; I need you now!" At that moment you no longer want the coffee, because you want to get over to your friend's house as fast as possible.

What happened in the above example is that you changed what you wanted – you changed your will. Does that mean you are a changed person? Of course not. A change in will does not constitute a change in essence. And so, on one level, as long as your will is consistent with your essence, there is no difference between what you want and who you are. However, that is not to say that they are always one and the same, because actualized will is interactive and changeable, whereas essence is not.

Concerning God, we have been told, "I am God, I do not change."[65]

God is absolute unity, totally perfect and self-contained, and He doesn't change. He doesn't get better, He doesn't get worse, He doesn't get larger or smaller. But, the will of God – or the light that comes from His infinite essence – creates, interacts with, and sustains various levels of change.

So the will of God had to undergo change, in terms of its manifestation, in order to make room for His creation. Parents have to do the same thing to allow their children to become individuals. We've all encountered mothers who smother their children, because they desire the best for them and wind up being overly protective. How important breathing room is to our well-being is reflected in our language – we say, "Don't crowd me," or "Give me space." In other words, we are telling each other, "Don't push your will on me too much. If you want me to exist, your will has to contract to make room for me, for my will, for my existence."

This is exactly what God did for His creation to exist, to have its own will.

The Kabbalists tell us that in creating the universe, God contracted His will, or put another way, He constricted the light of His infinite essence. When God did that, aspects of His light moved toward each other, densifying as they met and merging in a central place.[66]

 (An artist does something like this when he squints his eyes in order to focus and block out interference from peripheral vision, when trying to create an unimpeded context for what he desires to paint or bring to light.)

Once constricted and merged, those aspects of light

became a tiny densified dot surrounded by the light of God's infinite essence, of which it was once a part. Then God contracted the light of His infinite essence, in equal measure, away from this tiny dot. As He did so, a multi-dimensional vacated space filled with Divine nothingness was brought into existence. Within the context of that space, God created the totality of creation, from the highest spiritual rung to the central focal point of the physical world.[67]

Why are we calling this Divine nothingness? Why not just call it nothingness? Because this nothingness was brought about by the constriction of what once was the light of God's will, which means we can still sense God's vacated presence within it. That means that somebody encountering this vacated space can experience it as a great abyss, a place of hopelessness and despair, a context in which God is virtually absent, (as He must be, since otherwise there would be no place for the world). Or somebody encountering this vacated space can experience it as imbued with pure potential, a context for new beginning, a place of "no-thingness" out of which everything can evolve, the source of creation ex-nihilo.

So we have a notion of vacated space as a void, which is empty on the one hand in order for creation to exist, and yet, on the other hand, bears witness to God's vacated presence.

This may seem like a very peculiar way of putting things, but nevertheless the fact that you have a hole in the sand implies that somebody dug it and that there used to be sand in it.

This vacated space is very much like a womb, made to hold the totality of creation. Everything that God brought into existence and continues to nurture is contained within this womb of vacated space. Indeed, the vacated space may be seen as the archetypal "context" for the whole of existence. And, according to the Kabbalists, its influence reverberates at the core of every manifestation of context within creation.[68]But let us not forget that at the very center of this vacated space (this Divine nothingness) is a tiny, densified dot comprised of the light that preceded creation. That is to say, there is something of the primordial at the center and core of the context that allows for creation. And like a dot at the center of a sphere, its radii extend to all that exists.

Similarly, there is a dot of pure consciousness at the core of every person. Its radii extend to everything within the sphere of our existence. We become more and more consciously aware as we develop and mature. But the nature of pure consciousness before it becomes aware of anything at all remains elusive. This is like the nature of essential being, densified within creation, from which the powers of perception proceed. Yet, the sum total of those powers cannot begin to adequately describe the nature of consciousness from which they derive.

Thus it is interesting that the thing we are all most sure of in life is the fact of our own existence. And yet this fact can never be empirically substantiated – perhaps we are merely the by-products of some greater creation's dream. Subjective reality grounds us but does not remedy doubt.

Vacated Space in the "Here and Now"

My father was a schizophrenic. When I was a young child, I would come to the table, and he would say, "wash your hands." So I would go to the bathroom and wash my hands. And then he would say, "Let me see your hands … Well, they're still dirty. Go wash them again." So I would go wash them again. And then he would look at them a third time and say, "They're still dirty, wash them again." So I'd have to wash my hands three or four times before each meal, before he would pronounce my hands clean. Then, one day, when I was about eight years old, I went into the bathroom after he asked me to wash my hands, and I washed my hands scrupulously well. Then I came out, and of course he said, "Go back and wash them again." So I went back and I let the water run, but I didn't wash them. And then he sent me back a third time, and again I let the water run, but I didn't wash them. And after a while, he said, "Okay, now they're clean."

And from that moment I knew, with absolute certainty, that I had to remove myself from him in order to maintain my own sanity, my own sense of balance in the world. And, I managed to do that very well. My father's been dead for forty years, and every time I remember the space that I created in order to protect myself from his influence, I also remember his vacated presence.

That's the negative perspective. But in the case of God, it's positive. God created a vacated space – a space absent of Him, but bearing witness to His vacated presence – for our good.

God created the universe in that vacated space. But that space is never filled by what it contains. Indeed, aspects of that space continue to surround the entirety of creation made manifest in its midst. Were this not so, then all of creation would be overwhelmed and obliterated by the light of God's essence.[69]

That is, there would be nothing to separate and distinguish the creation from its Creator.

Indeed, all distinction derives from the vacated space. Concepts such as inner and outer, immanence and transcendence, creation and creator are only possible because of this space. Were the vacated space to be filled by God, then all creation would be absorbed into the oneness of His unity. The universe, every aspect of which is manifestation of God's will would then be overwhelmed by the infinite all-encompassing transcending power of its unified source. Imagine what would happen to a single drop of water trying to maintain an independent recognizable existence in the middle of the Atlantic Ocean.

Thus, there has to be an aspect to this vacated space, which is never filled by what it contains and continues to act as a buffer zone, so to speak, encompassing the universe and safeguarding its continued existence.

In our physical world, this aspect of vacated space may be detected in many situations. For example, why is it that two thoughts never flow together and merge like pudding? Where does one thought end and the other thought begin? The zone between streams of thought or streams of awareness is a reverberation of that original vacated space.

The Kabbalists teach us that this buffer zone – meaning the vacated space between the light of God's transcendent will (that exists outside His creation) and the immanent manifestations of that will (which inherently sustain His creation) – always remains the same. No matter what comes about in the universe, no matter how things may expand or multiply, no matter how much things change, they will always remain proportionately the same with respect to the vacated space. Indeed, the space meant to separate between immanence and transcendence, between creation and creator, will always remain the same.[70]

Hence in that original vacated space we find the archetypal beginnings of sacred space, which, according to the Sages, is never filled or diminished by what it contains.71 As a small child I had an experience which later helped me relate to the idea of vacated space in a personal way. I had been playing in a hallway off the kitchen, when I noticed, at the bottom of one of the walls, just above the baseboard, a small opening – a vacated space, if you will. Looking at it more closely, I was overwhelmed by a deep desire to put something inside, to fill that space no matter what.

I tried to insert my small fingers into the tiny opening, but my fingers, small as they were, were still too large. I got down on my hands and knees and peered into the space. All I could see was darkness. Looking up in frustration, I saw sitting nearby a solution to my dilemma – my father's toolbox. I picked up a small screwdriver and managed to insert the tip into the crack, but the rest of it was a little too thick and I couldn't force it in all the way. To remedy the problem, I picked up a hammer and gave the handle of the screwdriver a mighty whack with all my strength.

Suddenly, without warning, a stream of electrical sparks issued forth from the opening in the wall and the whole house went dark. Terrified, I began to scream hysterically, and my mother ran from the kitchen and swept me up in her arms, yelling that I could have been electrocuted.

For me, looking back, it was a revelatory experience. I had encountered transcending sparks of the infinite light that surely exists on the other side of darkness beyond the vacated space. At the same time I intuitively understood that not every space was meant to be filled, and those that were, weren't made to hold just anything. As I grew older I came to realize that vacated spaces as we encounter them in this world are either productive or non-productive. Productive space acts as a container holding or accentuating something other than itself. Non-productive space, however, should be completely annihilated or filled; it does not belong, like a tear in one's garment.

The kinds of space we confront are not always easy to identify. In conversation, for example, especially with people unfamiliar to ourselves, there tend to be lapses, vacated spaces, for us to deal with. Should such spaces be filled with new words and ideas or allowed to remain empty, accentuating the absence of dialogue?

Awkward silences may be alleviated by speech, but silence itself often provides a context for understanding beyond the place of words. Alternatively, the need to respond, at this particular time, might best be abandoned altogether, temporarily shifting the burden of communication to one's companion.

Or perhaps, one should speak incessantly, obliterating any and all space that allows for the possible disappointment associated with non-responsiveness.

Yet, despite the confusion that emanates from certain vacated spaces, there exists at the heart of each space a conceptual reality of Divine nothingness. It is this reality that constitutes the latent primal source of new beginning and healing.

With this in mind, we can confront the vacated space as it exists in ourselves, projecting our awareness to the Divinity at its core. In so doing, a context is established through which we begin to perceive our connection to God and are no longer overwhelmed while in the midst of His vacated presence. We experience inner wholeness, expansiveness and faith which derive from will compressed and unarticulated at the core of our being.

The Model of Paradox

The concept of vacated space – where God constricts

His will and removes His presence, in order that the universe be brought into existence as a creation of the Creator, but which is separate from the Creator Himself – is a paradox. The great Hassidic Master, Rebbe Nachman of Breslov,[72] and many other mystics, point this out and here is why:

On the one hand we learn from the Zohar[73] that there's no place empty of God, and that anything God creates must be sustained by His life-force. Thus, if the vacated space is a creation of God, and if every millimeter in that vacated space has to be sustained by God's life-force, then the vacated space is not empty of God. And if the vacated space is not empty of God, then there's no room for creation. So if creation exists, the vacated space must be empty, but that cannot be since nothing can exist without God's life-force to sustain it. That's the paradox.

Put another way, if the vacated space is a creation of God, it can't be sustained without the presence of God; but if God is present, then there's no room for the universe.

Some of the greatest Sages and Kabbalists have pondered this same dynamic in relation to God's foreknowledge and man's freedom of choice. And they have concluded that these two seemingly contradictory notions constitute a paradox that is essentially the same as that of the vacated space.[74] (Indeed, as we shall see, the paradox of vacated space is one of the great universal models explaining the tension that triggers the life-force.)

Just as the universe cannot exist unless the space is empty of God, while the space cannot exist unless it is nurtured by God, so too, human choice cannot exist unless it is empty of God's influence (i.e. His foreknowledge as we will explain), while nothing can exist not nurtured by God or beyond His ongoing influence (not even man's freedom of choice).[75]

This problem – which, we will soon see, applies to healing as well – can be stated more simply as follows:

If God is God – that is, if He is infinite and unified, and all knowledge is one with Himself, including knowledge that is finite – then God must know our choices before they are made. Indeed, God knows our choices, because they exist in Himself. Furthermore, if God's knowledge is one with Himself, then it cannot change, and if His knowledge is absolute, then it cannot be wrong.

Therefore, we can only choose what God already knows we will choose. But if that is true, then how can our choices be truly free and our own?

In an attempt to resolve this paradox one might say that God is outside of time; indeed, the time-space continuum was created by Him. Therefore, God knows all things in a constant state of now, and since the whole problem of His foreknowledge vs. freedom of choice is set within time, it doesn't apply to God! The problem with this approach is that the paradox is being posed concerning God's involvement with His creation on the level of immanence and not on the level of transcendence. We simply want to know how God, who is immanently involved with creation, can sustain the world and not interfere with it.

While some original insights and answers were offered by various sages and Kabbalists through the centuries, the conclusion that the majority reached is that it was possible for both God's foreknowledge and man's freedom of choice to exist simultaneously.[76]

Without a doubt, they said, man's choice is real and not illusionary, and man is ultimately responsible for each of his deeds. As the Book of Deuteronomy proclaims:

"I (God) call upon heaven and earth to witness against you this day, that I have set before you life and death, blessing and curse. Therefore choose life that you and your offspring may live…"[77] In other words, God is telling us that our choices are real with real consequences.

But in order for our choices to be real, God must restrict His knowledge of the future in such a manner as to allow for freedom of choice independent of His influence. As He did when He created the space for the universe to exist, God holds back and allows the world to continue, guided and influenced in accordance with the rules that govern creation which He Himself maintains.

In accordance with these rules, choice originates as a by-product of two factors:

First of all, there is choice that comes from the human condition (how I feel, what my context is, what my education happens to be, how I perceive and relate to my experience, etc.)

Secondly, there is ontological choice. Things are changing in the universe. As the prayer says: "God rejuvenates, in His goodness, every single day, the whole of creation." So every minute there are changes in the structure of the universe on all kinds of levels – from ever so slight molecular changes to the shifting of the positions of stars as the universe continues to expand (or so astronomers tell us.) And every time a change takes place, there are new possibilities that come into existence and thus new choices to be made. So choice is being manufactured in the universe from moment to moment.

But, ultimately, choice depends on one's inability to know. In other words, if I come to a crossroads and I know I am supposed to turn right, then unless I'm insane I am not going to turn left. But if I come to a crossroads, and I don't know if I am supposed to turn right or left, then I have a choice to make. The more profound my not knowing, the more profound my choice.

Therefore, the Kabbalists teach that God placed limitations on the human mind rendering it incapable of resolving the paradoxes we spoke of. For, if we were capable of understanding how it is possible for God, on the level of immanence, to know the future and for us to still have freedom of choice, then that knowledge would instantly deprive us of choice.

Since, as has been explained, the possibility of choice is ultimately dependent on our inability to know, then, if the possibility of choice is to be maintained, there must be something on each level of choice that is ultimately unknowable. And that something is itself the knowledge of how the paradox of choice can be resolved.[78]

This same rule applies to healing. There is paradox involved in this process as well. Both sides of this paradox must be dealt with if we are to open ourselves fully to the possibility of healing. On the one hand, we must know that our healing depends on what we are able to control and do for ourselves; on the other hand, we must accept that, at the very same time, our healing depends on our ability to go with the flow, saying yes to everything. As hard as that may be to understand, it is nevertheless how it is.

ABOUT THE AUTHOR

Rabbi Gedaliah Fleer is internationally well known as a teacher of Jewish philosophy, Hassidism and Kabbalah, as well as a story-teller. He has a unique ability to articulate complex esoteric concepts in a clear, direct, and understandable way. A teacher of profound intelligence, integrity and depth, he offers an amazing wealth of information and deep insights that can be applied to daily life.

Rabbi Fleer studied in the Mesivta Torah V'Daath and the Novardok Mussar Yeshiva and was ordained by the Breslover Yeshiva in Jerusalem. He and his wife, Rochel Bracha, live in Jerusalem, where Rabbi Fleer may be reached at (011-972-2) 623-5492 or jrbl18@yahoo.com for lectures, classes and seminars.

ENDNOTES

The following notations are meant primarily for the serious student or scholar of Kabbalah, one familiar with the Hebrew and Aramaic languages and traditional source materials.

Unfortunately, most of these sources have not been translated into English. Nevertheless, wherever possible – to make this material accessible to as broad range of audience as possible – I have tried to cite secondary sources in English translation.

I would like to point out that various reliable translations of the Hebrew Bible with Rashi commentary, the Midrash Rabba, the Talmud and even the Zohar – the chief work of the Kabbalah – are available at most well-stocked Jewish bookstores.

Generally speaking, the works of Rabbi Aryeh Kaplan and Rabbi Yitzchak Ginsburgh, well known in traditional Jewish circles, are a good place to start for anyone new to Kabbalah. Indeed, anyone wanting to know more about Kabbalistic or Hassidic doctrine and teaching will surely find their books an invaluable asset. Information about the publishers of their works can be found below; also see Rabbi Ginsburgh's website www.inner.org.

For English translation and commentary on the writings of Rebbe Nachman of Breslov, from whose teachings much of my thought process has evolved, one may write to Rabbi Chaim Kramer, Breslov Research Institute, POB 5370, Jerusalem, Israel, and also see www.breslov.org

1. All blessing or curse that comes from "above" is activated according to one's behavior "below" in this world. Zohar 3:31b; 3:105a.

2. Babylonian Talmud (which we will refer to henceforth by the initials T.B.) Berachot 5a.

3. T.B. Berachot 5a and Sanhedrin 99a.

4. See The Handbook of Jewish Thought, by Rabbi Aryeh Kaplan, Moznaim, 1992, Vol. 2, Ch. 19.

5. Pardes Rimonim, Shaar Erkhay HaKinuyim - "Makom"; The Handbook of Jewish Thought, Vol. 1, p. 10, para. 2:18, and note 21 ad loc.

6. Genesis 1:9.

7. Midrash Genesis Rabbah 5:7; T.B. Megillah 10b; T.B. Yoma 21a; Avot 5:7.

8. Genesis 28:12.

9. T.B. Chulin 60b: "What good is a candle in the light of day?" The word tihar means "light of day."

10. See The Courage to Create by Rollo May, W.W. Norton & Co., 1984, p. 157.

11. Psalms 94:9.

12. See *Healing Into Immortality* by Gerald Epstein, Bantam, 1994, p. 37.

13. Ibid, p. 16.

14. "Keeping a Quantum Kettle from Boiling" by I. Peterson, *Science News*, Vol. 136, No. 19, November 4, 1989.

15. T.B. Eruvin 13b; Jerusalem Talmud, Sotah 9; Shevet Mussar, Chapter 17.

16. See *The Jewish Way in Death and Mourning* by Rabbi Maurice Lamm, Jonathan David Publishing Co., 1969, p. 232, where the author quotes the Hebrew work, Gesher HaChaim by V.M. Tuckachinsky.

17. See the Jewish morning prayers: "In His goodness, He daily renews the act of creation." Also see Yad, Yesodey HaTorah 2:9; Zohar 3:31a, 3:225a; Lekutey Amarim (Tanya) Shaar HaYichud VeHaEmunah 2 (77b); T.B. Berachot 10a.

18. Lekutey Halakhot (Breslov) Orech Chaim, Pesach, Halakhah 7:2.

19. Lekutey Moharan 1:65:3.

20. See Midrash Genesis Rabbah 14:9; Deuteronomy Rabbah 2:9; Shaar HaGilgulim 1; Derekh HaShem

3:1:4; Inner Space by Rabbi Aryeh Kaplan, New York: Moznaim Publishing Co., 1990, p. 16.

21. Etz Chaim, Vol. 1, 6:5, (p. 84), Vol. 2 40:10 (p. 281), 40:12 (p. 285), 45:1 (p. 345); Nefesh HaChaim 2:17.

22. See Lekutey Moharan 1:65:3; and Innerspace by Rabbi Aryeh Kaplan, Moznaim, 1990, p. 16 and pp. 110-115.

23. Lekutey Moharan 1:22:5.

24. Midrash Tanchumah, Shemot 18, Korach 9; Rav Nissim Gaon on T.B. Berachot 32a; Ramchal, Hoker UmKubal (p. 4).

25. See The Mystery of Marriage by Rabbi Yitzchak Ginsburgh, Gal Einai Institute, 1999, pp. 191-193.

26. Lekutey Moharan 1:21:1-4.

27. Exodus33 :27

28. Midrash Genesis Rabbah 68:10. 28

29. Lekutey Moharan 1:282.

30. 2930 See Midrash Genesis Rabbah 14:9; Deuteronomy Rabbah 2:9; Shaar HaGilgulim 1; Derekh HaShem 3:1:4; Inner Space, p. 16.

31. 3031 Lekutey Moharan 1:65:4, and commentary Parparot LeChokhmah on this lesson.

32. 31Genesis 2:7

33. Job 32:8.

34. See Laws of Form by G. Spence-Brown, by Cognizer Co., 1994.

35. Etz Chaim, Vol. 1, 6:5, (p. 84), Vol. 2 40:10 (p. 281), 40:12 (p. 285), 45:1 (p. 345); Nefesh HaChaim 2:17.

36. What follows is a general description of how the neshamah interacts with chayah and yechidah. For details one must understand that the five levels of soul parallel the five spiritual universes, which in turn parallel the ten sefirot. (See Midrash Genesis Rabbah 14:9; Deuteronomy Rabbah 2:9; Shaar HaGilgulim 1; Derekh HaShem 3:1:4; Inner Space, p. 16. Having digested this information, see Lekutey Moharan 1:24:1-8.)

37. T.B. Niddah 30b.

38. Mishnat Hassidim, Masechet Briyat Adam Kadmon, Chapters 1-2.

39. T.B. Berachot 10a.

40. Psalms 33:6.

41. Psalms 104:30.

42. Genesis 2:7.

43. Rebbe Nachman of Breslov, 1772-1810, was the great-grandson of the Baal Shem Tov, the founder of the Hassidic Movement; this quotation comes from Lekutey Moharan, Lesson 8:1.

44. Genesis 1:3-26.

45. Zohar 3:123b; also see Ramban on Genesis 2:7; Shefa Tal, introduction (4c); Tanya, Lekutey Amarim 2 (p.5b).

46. Midrash Genesis Rabbah 5:1.

47. Exodus 31:17.

48. Oral Tradition among Breslover Hassidim, quoted by Rabbi Elya Chaim Rosen.

49. Tikuney Zohar, Tikun 5.

50. Sichat HaRan 308.

51. Sichat HaRan 16; Lekutey Moharan 2:5:2 with commentary Parparot LeChokhmah. Also, see commentary Biyur Halikutim on this lesson, and Zohar 1:141b.

52. Kabbalistically speaking, the yechidah aspect
    of soul is sourced in and nurtured by the sefirah
    of keter, the highest of the sefirot. Keter
    represents God's altruistic desire to bestow
    goodness upon His creation. God's goodness, as it
    manifests within the level of keter, is
    unconditional and is ultimately the life force
    for all that exists. The light of keter flows into
    the sefirah of chokhmah, which is directly
    beneath it and in which is sourced the chayah
    aspect of soul. Chayah is reinvigorated whenever
    chokhmah receives an influx from yechidah. Next
    in line, the neshamah aspect of soul is sourced in
    the sefirah of binah. The neshamah is associated
    with breath and is the source of all sound; it
    is accessed by an actual audible scream. However,
    when focused upward the neshamah emits a silent
    scream which arouses the sefirah of chokhmah
    Once aroused, chokhmah flows into and
    reinvigorates the sefirah of binah which in
    turn affects the neshamah. However, when the
    breath sourced in neshamah is focused
    downward, it becomes a melody without words
    and then it nurtures the ruach aspect of soul
    Ruach is associated with the next six sefirot,
    from chessed to yesod, which comprise the
    realm of emotions known as Zair Anpin. When
    ruach extends downward and gives of its light
    to the nefesh, it becomes a melody with words.

However, the nefesh, which is associated with the sefirah of malkhut, is manifested by words clearly articulated. See: Zohar Ibid 2:20a; Pardes Rimonim, Shaar Erkhay Ha Kinuyim "Tza'akah"; Etz Chaim 22:1(p. 307); Mevo Shearim 5:1:14

53.   Tanya, Lekutey Amarim, Chapter 7 (p. 11); Etz Chaim 50:10 (vol. 2, p. 407); Pirkey Rabbi Eliezer 34 (p. 79b).53

54.   Proverbs 20:27.

55.   Psalms 4:8.

56.   Psalms 97:11.

57.   Lekutey Moharan, Lesson 5:3.

58.   T.B. Berachot 59a.

59.   Zohar 235b.

60.   Ibid.

61.   Song of Songs 4:15.

62.   Emunoth VeDeyoth 3:0; Shevil Emunah ad loc. 3:0:1.

63.   Emunoth VeDeyoth ibid; T.B. Sanhedrin 39b, Rashi ad loc. S.v. Oder; T.B. Menachot 53b; Esther Rabbah 10:15; Akedath Yitzchak 60.

64. Etz Chaim, Derush Egulim VeYosher 2; Mavo Shaarim 1:1; Lekutey Moharan 1:49.

65. See Innerspace, pp. 13, 23-24, 120-125; Hoker U'mkubal by Rabbi Moshe Chaim Luzzato, Bnei Brak: Bais Hasofer, pp. 4-5; Derekh Mitzvotekha, Emunat Elokuth 6 (51a).

66. Malachi 3:6.

67. See Packhad Yitzchak, commentary on Otzrot Chaim, published by Rabbi I. Benzecry, 1988, Ch. 69.

68. Etz Chaim 1:1:2 (p. 27); Shaar Hakdamot, p. 14; Mevo Shearim 1:1:1.

69. See: Pardes Rimonim, Shaar Erkhay HaKinuyim - "Makom"; The Handbook of Jewish Thought, Vol. 1, p. 10, para. 2:18, and note 21 ad loc. See also: Innerspace, pp. 124-125, 216 note 19.

70. Shefa Tal, introduction (4d); Lekutey Moharan 1:64:1; Zohar 3:47b; T.B. Chulin 60a, 60b; Yalkut Shimoni 1:39b.

71. Packhad Yitzchak, commentary on Otzrot Chaim, p. 8.

72. Midrash Genesis Rabbah 5:7; T.B. Megillah 10b; T.B. Yoma 21a; Avot 5:7.

73. Lekutey Moharan 1:64:1,2.

74. Zohar 3:225a; Tikuney Zohar 57 (91b), 70 (122b).

75. Kellaley Chokhmat HaEmet, introduction, p. 2a; YAD, Teshuvah 5:5; Emunoth VeDeyoth 4:4; Pardes Rimonim 4:9; Akedath Yitzchak 2 (151a); Teshuvoth Rivash 119; Lekutey Moharan 1:21:45.

76. Lekutey Halachot (Breslov) Yoreh Deah, Divarim HaYotzim Min HaChay, Halakhah 4.

77. See endnotes 73 and 74 immediately above.

78. Deuteronomy 30:19-20.

79. Lekutey Halachot (Breslov), Yoreh Deah, Divarim HaYotzim Min HaChay 4:39:40.

Made in the USA
Middletown, DE
10 September 2019